ECONOMICS OF RURAL TRANSPORT

SABITA GUHA

2018

Daya Publishing House®

A Division of

Astral International Pvt. Ltd.

New Delhi - 110 002

First Published, 1991
Reprinted, 2018

ISBN: 978-81-7035-102-3 (Hardbound)

Published by : **Daya Publishing House®**
A Division of
Astral International Pvt. Ltd.
– ISO 9001:2008 Certified Company –
4736/23, Ansari Road, Darya Ganj
New Delhi-110 002
Ph. 011-43549197, 23278134
E-mail: info@astralint.com
Website: www.astralint.com

In the Memory of
my Father
the Late Prof. B.C. Guha

FOREWORD

Theory enlightens choice. Since economic decisions imply choice, economists have developed theories and tools for enlightened decision-making. The usefulness of applying such theories and tools in discriminating among alternative decisions, particularly among microlevel projects, is now widely admitted. In India too, such exercises are now a common practice.

However, at the time when the authoress started her exercises, as reported in the present volume, most doctoral dissertations in economics presented to the Indian universities, had not yet shed their largely descriptive or speculative character. Hence, the book deserves a place among the pioneering efforts to make university dissertations in India more meaningful.

It is gratifying to note that Dr. Guha was not carried away by the novelty of the new theories and tools, which constitute the basis of the bulk of her present work. The fact that she kept her feet firmly grounded is proved by her discourse in Part III, in which she expounds short-cut methods warranted when required data are not readily available, but decisions cannot wait. In the case of rural transport in India, such eventualities are perhaps the rule, rather than the exception. The book should prove useful to the beginners in the job of decision-making on roads, rural roads in particular.

Santosh Bhattacharyya
Ph. D. (ECON. LOND.)
Formerly, – Vice Chancellor
University of Calcutta

PREFACE

This book attempts to provide an analytical framework for project appraisal in the transport sector in rural areas. Transport provides the life line of an economy. Hence the demand for a viable network of transport is almost universal. As a consequence, investment decisions in this sector is sometimes hasty and not always cost effective. Moreover, there are different modes of transport and in most cases investment on alignments is undertaken in the public sector. Such investment cannot be justified by profitability criterion. Investment on road is a case in point.

In our country, in the present era road is the principal mode of transport in rural areas. Water transport played a significant role earlier and is still made use of in selected areas. But there is a dirth of decision making criteria for guiding investment on rural roads. Apart from making some general observations on the weightages to be given to population and agricultural productivity, the experts have not gone into the question of efficient utilisation of resources in this sector.

Here is an honest endeavour for removing the deficiency at the theoretical plane. The book has four sections. In Part I, the social cost benefit criterion is discussed and its application for evaluating a rural road project is demonstrated with reference to a particular road section. In Part II, the regression technique is presented in a nut shell and it is made use of to assess the effects of development of a rural road network on its catchment area. In Part III, the weighted rating method is presented and a case study using the method shows how easily the criterion can be adopted for taking speedy decision. Finally, in Part IV, the role of water transport in an area having natural advantage is discussed and a balanced approach towards development of rural transport is advocated.

The book is an adaptation and assimilation of author's Ph.D. thesis (Calcutta University) and subsequent post doctoral work (Institute of Economic Growth, Delhi University). The author will feel her painstaking work justified if it arouses the curiousity of research workers in the field of transport.

Sabita Guha
State Planning Board,
Government of West Bengal

CONTENTS

INTRODUCTION

Transport Planning in Rural Areas

A rural transport network is to provide an all pervasive and viable service in an area which is to form an integral part of a self regulating village community. Of course, in the present day society, it is rather difficult to define a rural area. Population, degree of industrialisation, extent of civic amenities and such other items may be used for preparing a composite index of urbanisation. However, in a country like India, with heavy dependence on primary sector and with little civic amenities as well as low level of technology, the rural areas are more or less easily identifiable and cover vast tract of land. Most of those areas, again, suffer from paucity of transport and communication facilities. During my wide travel in rural areas I have often come across villagers who feel that state help is needed in two spheres–irrigation and transport. They are competent to look after rest of their needs.

Coming to transport, we find the overall transport service to be provided in an area is to be adequate in response to people's demand for carrying surplus output of the region to desirable market as also bringing necessities from their choicest place. Socially, it should be adequate in terms of people's journey demand for work, family necessity, social intercourse as well as pleasure trips. Economically, it is to be viable in the sense that its rate of utilisation is sufficient to justify the cost of providing the service.

But there are certain difficulties inherent in transport planning. Transport services are extremely heterogeneous and a unified control of different modes is almost impossible since the system involves a number of small decisions. Moreover the need for transport services is conditioned by the level of economic activity in general which is continuously changing. But transport infrastructure cannot be adjusted to changing needs too quickly. Just as surplus transport capacity cannot be stored for future utilisation so also transport bottlenecks cannot be removed overnight. Therefore, the entire programme is to be based on proper forecasting of future activity level, taking into account the extant socio-economic condition.

Providing a viable transport infrastructure for a particular economy is not an easy task. One has to decide on the size of transport sector vis-a-vis other sectors of the economy. Since different modes of transport may be made available in a particular area, the problem of intersectoral balance looms large. Achieving inter-sectoral balance at a macro-level say, for the entire country is really a stupendous job. However, the choice at the micro-level is relatively easier as the available alternatives are limited. Let us take the case of rural India, where even now people have to move about on foot along kuchha roads and animal-driven-vehicles are the only mode of transport. In riverine areas, country boats operate along navigable rivers and canals carrying both passengers and commodities. So, for such isolated area units, having little or no infrastructural facilities transport planning may simply mean formulation of a road network plan which will connect the area with market centres, urban centres, rail heads so forth and so on. Again introduction of mechanised boats along selected waterways may have a major beneficial effect in such a rural economy in terms of time saving and reduction of accident. Water transport can be effectively made use of only in case of perennial waterways. But road transport has a universal appeal, since some form of road network is always there in every human habitation.

Road as the Principal Mode of Rural Transport

The term road has a very wide denotation. Any strech of land joining two termini is a road. It may be quite narrow, muddy and short (as is common within villages). It may be wide, high levelled, metalled and long winding. Sometimes streets, highways and such other terms are used to denote different categories of roads. Broadly speaking, a road may be defined as a convenient pathway over which vehicles and pedestrians can move freely and cover the distance between the starting point and the ultimate destination. The two termini may be thousand miles apart or they may be quite close to each other. The vehicles and pedestrians moving along the road together constitute the total volume of traffic. Traffic has a right of way over the road or enjoys the privilege of using the road according to law or custom.

The same consideration holds for other modes of transport. In fact provision of transport services involve two steps — chalking out the alignment which decision normally rests with a central authority and supply of rolling stock, where private investment is quite common. Take the case of each one of the four modes of transport — airways, waterways, railways, roadways. The alignments are designed and controlled by the state and the state grants rights of way to the vehicles moving along the routes, while vehicles may be operated both by private and state organisations.

In rural areas in our country, we cannot afford the luxury of airways. Railways traverse through length and breadth of the country, but interconnection with remote areas are not cost effective. So rural areas have to depend on roadways and waterways. Of these, the former involves investment on alignment while the latter does not require it. State involvement in the second case is therefore nominal. Ferries are managed privately and charging is easy. Administration comes to the picture for control and regulation which are often quite loose. The case is rather different for roads. Investment on alignment is a must and the fund is to be provided by the public sector. Such investment takes place at all levels of government — central, regional and local. The amount of investment depends on specification of roads which is again guided by the traffic that it expects to bear. So the need for investment appraisal is widely felt in this sector.

To start with a functional classification of roads is necessary. Some roads are built to serve a limited purpose, namely that of providing access to residential buildings, shoping centres etc. These are land access roads satisfying needs of a locality and normally they have lower specifications. Of course sometimes there may be high grade local roads mainly running through urban areas and carrying heavy traffic.

A second major type of roads is called an arterial. It usually connects important centres lying at a distance from one another. They carry a larger volume of traffic. Still travel is generally swifter along arterials. Providing land access facility is of not so much importance to arterials whose primary object is to arrange for smooth flow of long distance traffic. Feeder roads branch out of arterials, thereby connecting a centre with a long distance road.

A third type, express way, is rapidly making headway. Its sole purpose is to serve vehicles in motion and it does not bother at all with land access facilities. Because of the pressure of traffic on such roads express ways are carefully designed with fully separated directional traffic and with no intersections at grade with other streets. Such express ways make possible uninterrupted, fast movement of motor vehicles and ensure speed. But naturally these are costly roads and they become economic only when the pressure of fast moving traffic is heavy.

Within these broad categories, roads may be of different specifications. However, roads are usually divided into three general classes according to their specification standard. These are earth road, gravel road and pavement. The first two together may be further grouped under the broad heading of unmetalled road, while the third variety is popularly known as metalled road. In case of metalled road, crust of pavement is not the same everywhere. The traffic bearing capacity of a road depends among other conditions on the thickness of the crust. Metalled roads are serviceable under all weather and motor vehicles have easy access on them. Unmetalled roads, even when they are sufficiently wide, are not always capable of carrying heavy motor vehicles. Roads which are expected to carry long distance traffic and ensure smooth flow of traffic have got to be metalled. A road infrastructure in a rural area is to be built up by constructing metalled arterials interconnected with metalled or unmetalled local roads, depending on soil and weather conditions. The Express Ways run through fringe areas and are not normally integrated in the system.

Differences in road specifications give rise to differences in costs of construction and maintenance. The higher the standard of specification, the greater will be the cost of construction.

Cost of maintenance is related to the rate of utilisation of road as also the specification standard. If the initial investment is high because of higher standard of specification, maintenance cost is comparatively low. Capacity to bear traffic in such cases is quite high. The projected traffic pattern as also availability of resources should determine road specification. One thing is convenient for road planning, once an alignment is demarcated rest of the work can be done in stages. Also an unmetalled road can be upgraded if traffic so demand. But it is necessary to chalk out a road net work in conformity with the optimum land use pattern of an area. So the State authority comes into the picture both at planning and at execution stage.

Investment in Roads

One of the major responsibilities of the state now a days is to provide for social wants. R.A Musgrave[1] has given the following definition of social want. 'Social wants are those wants satisfied by services that must be consumed in equal amounts by all. People who do not pay for the service cannot be excluded from the benefits that result: and since they cannot be excluded from the benefits, they will not engage in voluntary payments'. The market mechanism fails in such cases and private sector will not come forward for satisfying social wants. Public sector will not be in a position to justify its commitment easily by tangible return since charging is difficult. Still, it must have certain tools of analysis enabling it to determine the extent to which such social wants are to be satisfied. Otherwise, inefficiency will creep in and resources will be wasted.

Clearly transport services belong to the category of social want. Investment in a road project or a rail project is of the nature of an expenditure on the creation of a durable good. It is a more or less permanent asset and yields continuous return or benefit. But in order that the flow of return may remain unimpaired for a length of time, the asset has to be kept in good condition. A recurrent expenditure is to be incurred for the purpose. The different types of motor vehicles in vogue now a days require broad surfaced roads for speedy and smooth travel. Construction of such roads involves huge investment cost.

Maintenance cost is not negligible either. Hence in the public sector, investment in road is considerable in almost every economy now a days.

Investment decision in respect of roads however, appears to be difficult as charging for road services is not at all feasible. Still, because of the tremendous social, economic as also administrative significance of roads, considerable amount of public investment has to be channelled towards this sector. Again, allocation within the sector has to be made weighing the importance of different road sections against one another. For example a list of projects may be prepared for the entire sector depending on the general idea of community's requirements as revealed in the projected traffic pattern. Since all of them cannot be taken up at a time, prioritisation is necessary. But this is true for all major investments.

Creation of transport facility absorbs a large portion of public investment. But state cannot charge directly for chalking out an alignment. However, it is costly in case of roadways and railways. While rolling stocks is also under state in most cases for railways, road vehicles are operated by private owners.

Construction of road is more or less a simple activity and can be undertaken by utilising local resources. Normally in rural areas people always clamour for good roads. The socio-economic impact of road can be abstructly justified rather easily. Hence quite often projects are taken up without careful scrutiny. Sometimes, unusual delay takes place during implementation stage, since difficulties crop up only after the project is launched. Thus capital remains blocked up, quick decision leads to wastage. So it is all the more necessary that there should be some way of checking the desirability or otherwise of a road project.

Roads are necessary for the traffic that they bear. Therefore, whenever the state undertakes construction of a road, the executing agency should form an idea about the traffic that the road section is expected to bear. Standard of specification will have to be decided on the basis of traffic projection and investment level will be decided accordingly.

Traffic, in its turn, depend on the existing level of economic activity as also on the future prospect of expanding activity level. Economic activity is likely to expand when the region has unutilised economic resources. Such regions should get preference in road planning. A road by itself cannot produce any tangible product which can be priced in the market. Its usefulness lies in opening up production centres. Hence economic potential of the catchment area has to be carefully studied before taking up a project. The greater the economic potential, the higher will be the rate of utilisation of road surface. Investment decisions are interrelated. The bad effect of a decision in one sector is quite often transmitted to other sectors. If a road system is built in a haphazard way production potential of the catchment area will not be fully and properly utilised. Hence, particular road projects are to be taken up after careful economic assessment in relation to the entire road system. Efficient planning of road network will not only solve communication problem but also ensure economic prosperity. A quantitative analysis is always a better guide than qualitative statements in investment decisions. Theoretically, different approaches may be developed and the models are to be made flexible enough so that they can be fitted to particular situations.

Decision Making in Public Sector

In transport sector, investment is undertaken both in public as well as in private sector, though their relative shares may be different in different countries. Those economies which are bent on acheiving progress in a planned way try to dovetail the two sectors. In capitalist or mixed economies, a sizable portion of modes of transports are owned and operated by private investors in their individual capacity. Charging is possible for using a particular mode of transport, be it motor vehicle, boat or aeroplane. The decisions are decentralised and follow rules of competitive market. Any elementary student of economics knows that decentralised economic activities in the private sector are normally guided by profitability consideration. For example, a rational entrepreneur will undertake projects yielding profit and will reject those involving less. He will try to maximise his profit by equalising marginal revenue and marginal cost. The criterion m.r. = m.c. can be applied when output is divisible and production follows the law of increasing cost. The same is true in the service sector. When production of commodity or supply of service comes under private sector, the state may interfere from time to time to correct imbalance in distribution or to ensure full employment of resources and manpower. In some cases state has to participate directly, e.g., when outputs are not divisible activities relating to them cannot be decentralised. Measures relating to defence, maintenance of law and order, stability of money value, taxation, etc., are best looked after by the central agency, namely, state. Some other services like education, communication, etc., may also be provided by the state in the interest of the community. Again, some forms of production or distribution of commodities such as energy, water, steel, mineral oil may be entrusted to public enterprises because of their external effects or because of increasing returns. Among these categories of goods and services, charging is possible in some cases, but not in others. In some other cases like education though charging is possible it may not be desirable under given social condition. Hence allocation of resources in these spheres has to be carefully determined. New techniques have to be adopted for the purpose.

Left to itself, marginal cost pricing is a sound principle and a golden rule for practical policy framing. But the trouble is, money cost does not always reflect social cost and monetary return, social benefit. So if we are to think in terms of social welfare, the old analysis has to be supplemented by new ideas and monetary costs and gains have to be adjusted accordingly. Moreover, when state provides for group wants, i.e., a service which is consumed in equal amounts by all, the above mentioned principle cannot be applied at all. A major difficulty crops up — since individuals cannot be made to pay directly for the service their individual preferences cannot be ascertained in the market. This difficulty is just relevant in case of road services. It is an essential service for the community. But how to build up a socially desirably and economically viable system?

The general outline of goals set for public sector projects is often too abstract and it is not easy to assess how far a single activity is going to fulfil such an objective. But a quantitative criterion is expected to examine a project objectively. It serves double purpose. By applying this criterion a planner can choose comparatively more desirable projects out of a long list and determine relative priority of different proposals. At the same time he can judge the efficiency of a project already executed and prescribe remedies for faulty steps undertaken. Of course the criterion may not be fully reliable. Still it provides a check against misuse of funds in public sector.

In practical sphere, while formulating a programme not much economic acumen is needed for priority determination. The main areas needing care for purposes of development are more or less predetermined. And no economist can claim to devise a formula which will just balance the marginal benefit derived from the last unit of expenditure on one sector against that derived from another unit on a second sector, under the same circumstances. Apart from claiming that health, education transport, etc., are all important sectors in the economy and deserve to be properly looked after, a planner can do no better than determine their relative shares within the framework of investment planning rather arbitrarily and intutively. But he will be able to do justice to this assignment if he is provided with tools of analysis to examine the projects that he is going to recommend. To overcome this difficulty he will have to be equipped with techniques of project evaluation so that allocation of resources may ensure efficiency.

The problem of project selection may assume different forms. For example, it may assume the form of selection of twenty projects out of a hundred proposals, for immediate initiation. If the projects are to be undertaken under a budgetary constraint cost estimates will play a major role in the process of selection and techniques will be determined accordingly. The costing data will have to be supplemented by a rough estimate of total area and population to be benefited by each one of these projects. Next, one single project may be executed in different ways. For example, canals may be excavated in different directions from a single reservoir. Road or railway authority may have the option of choosing between slightly different alignments, so forth and so on. The aim will naturally be to select that system of canals which will be in a position to supply water to largest area within a given cost structure. Similarly, in case of roadways or railways the choice of alignment will be related to the number of people who will be in a position to enjoy the facility.

Project Appraisal

Sophisticated models have been constructed for studying the impact of improvement in different public sector projects including transport on overall economic activity, both at macro micro level. I may mention two such studies on transport which aim at an integrated approach. Prof. Tinbergen first presented a highly sophisticated theoretical analysis in this sphere in an article[2] published in the Review of Economics and Statistics. Bos and Koyck later developed the idea further[3] during the middle of this century. Both studies use input-output models to assess the overall increase in national output consequent on an improvement of transport. The economy is divided into separate geographical entities being closely interrelated. Each unit is purchasing the products of other units. Therefore any change in transport cost has its impact on the demand supply condition and price structure of each product of each unit. The procedure consists in setting up the model in terms of an assumed 'existing set up' and then on the basis of a projected road improvement reducing transport cost by a certain unit, finally studying the effect of the reduction in transport cost on the total production of the economy. The method is one of comparative statics which consists in effecting a comparison of the national product between two hypothetical positions in the economy 'with and without' road improvement. The two articles try to establish the point that total benefit produced by road improvement is much higher than the reduction in transport costs consequent on it. But in order that such a model be used in macro analysis within practical sphere we need an inventory of detailed price and commodity data on a regional base. The studies also neglect the effects of road improvement on passenger transport.

Instead of thinking on a global term, in case of rural transport the need of project analysis in a disaggregative way is much greater. The cost benefit analysis may be effectively used in this sphere in a traditional way since it is an accepted appraisal technique for projects where commercial profitability fail to guide the decision making process. Hence is its popularity in assessing public sector projects specially irrigation and transport.

The economic effects of a project in the transport sector, say those of a road are often varied and far reaching. Logically, the economic reorganisation that takes place in the catchment area due to the opening of a road should be fully assessed in order to have an idea of social benefit. But for practical purposes a simpler tactics may be adopted, namely, measurement of benefit accruing to traffic in general, both existing ones as well as new additions. These benefits can be set against project cost to determine the desirability or otherwise of the project.

Harvard[4] economists developed a series of simulation models for transport planning. The transport network of a country is taken as a whole and the impact of a single new project is sought to be judged in relation to the existing network as also to other new projects. According to this approach, isolated project by project analysis is often one sided and has a limited value. A system analysis takes an all comprehensive view. The model envisaged by this group takes into account all the principal transport modes and tries to project the pattern of commodity flows over the transport network. The direct effect of any improvement in transport is either a reduction in cost, or an improvement in quality of the service, or both. These effects will next be transmitted to the economy and produce changes in important variables like outputs, wages, prices, etc. The model may be used to assess the overall impact on the economy, if a broad campus is envisaged. It can also provide answers to questions of local and regional importance. Flexibility is claimed to be its outstanding virtue. But here also data base is to be immensely strengthened even if a limited use of the tool is to be made.

The effects of improvement of road on production, price, employment etc. can be ascertained through simple regression analysis more easily. Though the exact magnitude of variation cannot be obtained in this way, but it can be proved that a positive relation exists between these variables and road improvement even if the locality served by the road is small and rather isolated.

Since it is generally accepted that transport projects are to be in conformity of the present and future activity level of the economy, they can be formulated taking into account certain relevant economic variables like population, major occupation of the people, main product produced in the region so forth and so on. These variables may be weighed and a composite index derived for selecting transport project. In the absence of strong data base, such an approach is quite helpful at a micro level in a rural economy. In the ensuing chapters, we shall present different analytical framework one after another and these will be followed by practical demonstrations.

REFERENCES

1. R.A. Musgrave, *Public Finance*, Ch. 1 Sec. - B.
2. J. Tinbergen, The appraisal of road construction. *Review of Economics & Statistics*, August, 1957.
3. Bos & Koyck, Appraisal of road construction projects. *Review of Economics & Statistics*, February, 1961.
4. J.R. Meyer (ed.), Techniques of Transport Planning, Vol. VI.

PART - 1

PROJECT APPRAISAL – CASE OF A SINGLE ROAD SECTION

1

COST BENEFIT ANALYSIS

Three Variants of Cost Benefit Analysis

Investment decisions, be it in the public or private sector, involves some sort of planning which takes into consideration probable returns from the project. In the private sector, market mechanism normally does the trick of project selection and profitability calculation dominates planning process. But in the public sector, this approach does not always hold good. Profit calculations relating to a particular project may not tally with the idea of social benefit. Then, in some cases charging is not at all possible for example, defence service, maintenance of law and order etc. Again in some other cases which we normally call welfare activities, supply of free service or under pricing is justifiable from society's point of view. Health, education, communication belong to this category. Free schooling up to a certain stage, free beds in hospitals, low pricing of postcards, envelopes etc. have been taken for granted. The costs on these accounts are to be justified on social consideration, the principle of marginal cost pricing cannot be followed in such cases.

Transport services occupy a peculiar position. There are sophisticated modes of transport like aeroplane, luxury buses, luxury railway coaches etc. High charges have to be paid for utilising their services. But the same principle does not hold for every transport facility. However arrangements have to be made for their smooth flow of all types of traffics along demarcated routes and terminal facilities have to be created for most of the vehicles. Investment on these accounts may not be easily justified in terms of prospective return. But they are essential from the point of view of the society. In rural areas we are generally restricted to two modes — these are roadways and waterways. No investment is needed for chalking out the alignment of waterways. The terminal facilities are mostly inadequate, being constructed as cheaply as possible by the ferry operators who run the service in private sector with a profit motive. The problem arises in case of roads where investment is to be incurred in the public sector and charging of road users is not possible. There may be a few exceptions like collection of the toll tax at the entry point of a bridge. The road user tax paid by motor vehicles may be regarded as the earning of the road sector. But the earning can hardly be intercepted for a particular road section. Moreover investment on road is not always financed out of proceeds from road user taxes. Hence a separate approach is to be developed for analysing investment on road. Since roads are of different specification and investment requirements vary with the standard to be attained, the method of analysis should be flexible enough to do justice to different variants. This leads us to the choice of cost benefit analysis for appraisal of road project. Cost benefit analysis is often adopted to justify public investment of the type in which charging is not possible or in which project decisions are not to be guided solely by the prospect of financial return. Though the technique can be used easily in projects with measurable returns, it is often applied in cases where imputed returns are calculated to ascertain social benefit.

The genesis of cost benefit technique can be traced back to the msb = msc rule of welfare economics. The analysis is mainly applied at the project level, when decentralisation of economic decision is necessary. Such decisions are undertaken on the basis of profit and loss calculation in private sector. Profit or loss is the difference between amount received through sale of a product and amount spent for procuring the product. These receipts and expenditures will correspond to social gain and social cost only under restrictive assumptions. It tries to adjust actual receipts and expenditures in such a way as to make them reflect real benefit and real cost to the society. The final shape of the criterion will depend on the nature of the project and the purpose of appraisal. The main advantage of this type of analysis is its flexibility. In general, the process entails identification of all benefits and costs associated with a single project and measurement of each one of them in terms of what it may add to or subtract from social product. This is of course a highly abstract analysis and we shall presently discuss the safeguards to be taken to arrive at reliable estimates of social cost and social benefit. Once these are obtained, they may be balanced against each other by subtracting costs from benefits or by dividing benefits by costs or some other suitable devices.

Normally, we get three methods of comparison in the literature on cost benefit analysis. The first is net present value method. Algebraically it is given as $\Sigma (B_n - C_n) / (1 + i)^n$ when B_n and C_n denote streams of benefits and costs, beginning from the start of the project and coming to the end of the life period, n stands for life period of the project and i the rate of discount for bringing all benefits and costs to the starting point at which the decision is to be taken. The alternative having the greatest present value is apparently the most desirable. Of course the net present value (NPV) will not be of much help unless and until we get a more or less reliable series covering a long period of time. Moreover such a technique tends to favour projects which are large in absolute terms, have large initial benefit and a rising cost stream with a low initial cost. Net benefit peters out in the end but the cumulative figure is handsome.

Next, we may think in terms of a rate of return on investment. The rate may be calculated by expressing total annual return (preferably minus running cost) as a percentage to total investment. The more sophisticated version consists in deducing a rate of discount which will equate the sum of annual discounted benefits to the amount invested. In other words this may be expressed in the form $\Sigma B_n/(1 + r)^n = I$, where n is the life period, B_n the benefit estimate at nth point of time and I total investment. The equation is to be solved for the value of 'r' which is called internal rate of return — a measure of desirability of the project. Naturally, the higher the value of 'r' the greater is the acceptability of the project. However, a unique value of 'r' may not be easily obtained. Multiple solutions are likely to occur if annual net benefits are alternatively positive and negative. Moreover application of different formulations may lead to different sets of choices.

The third formulation consists in calculating benefit cost ratio which is more akin to NPV calculation. When NPV is positive benefit cost ratio is normally higher than one. In fact the investment will be marked desirable if actually the ratio is higher than one. A detailed discussion of this version is available in Otto Eckstein's 'Water Resource Development'. In its simplest form the ratio is thus presented.

$$\sum_{t=1}^{T} B\sim/\sim(1+i)^t \;/\; \sum_{t=1}^{T} \frac{O}{(1+i)^t} + K,$$

where

B = benefit received annually as defined by agency practice
O = operating, maintenance and routine replacement costs incurred annually
K = fixed investment i = rate of interest
t = amortization period.

In the numerator, the ratio places the sum total of a fixed value of benefit through period of time and uses discounted values. In the denominator the sum of the discounted values of annual cost is added to the fixed investment.

Instead of taking the ratio of total benefit to total cost, annual benefit and cost concepts may also be introduced. The ratio in fact has been subsequently put on an annual basis. But this formulation suffers from certain drawbacks. K is taken as a lump sum and the influence of time on this item has not been taken account of. Just as flows of benefit and operation costs are discounted back to the starting point of the project, investment cost should be subjected to the same treatment. For investment normally spreads over a period of time. Moreover in this analysis gross benefit is compared to sum total of capital and recurring costs. But it is better to take O in the numerator. For logically in such an analysis investment cost is to be taken as the base against which the net benefit is measured. Again B and O may not be constant through time. B may be low at the initial stage. It may gather momentum as the project is in operation for a while. Similarly, O may increase as the project gets older. Taking note of these limitations, a second formulation is sought to be presented in the following para.

Retaining the earlier symbols, the ratio may be put in a slightly different form. In the numerator, gross benefit is replaced by net benefit i.e. O goes up. If we suppose benefits as also recurring costs to be changing and denote them by B_t and O_t then the sum total of net benefit accruing to the project for its entire life period is given by

$$\sum_{t=1}^{n} (B_t - O_t),$$

where n stands for the life period. In various projects the rate of change of benefit may be fairly guessed and O remains the same for a considerable length of time. Hence B_ts and O_ts may not have to be estimated afresh each year. Sometimes it may so happen that B and O remain actually constant for a period of time. But the sum total of flow of net benefits in the above expression gives generalised version of such estimates. In order that it may conform to a particular point of time the annual components are to be discounted back to the year at which benefit cost comparison is to be made. Similarly, investment cost is not to be treated as a whole. Such investment normally spreads over a period of time, each component is to be discounted back to the reference year and the sum total of discounted values is to be taken at the point of comparison. Normally, the technique is applied at the formulation stage to test the desirability or otherwise of the project. Hence, the year of starting the project may serve as the reference year. In that case taking q to be the gestation period and n the life period of the project, the ratio may simply be put in the form—

$$\sum_{t=q+1}^{q+n} (B_t - O_t)(1 + i)^{-t} \Big/ \sum_{t=1}^{q} (K_t (1 + i)^{-t}.$$

If this ratio is greater than 1 (one) we may conclude that the project is beneficial for the economy. Thus the method of benefit cost anaylsis as outlined above consists in taking the ratio of reliable estimates for sum total of net benefit to total investment cost at a particular point of time, taking the range of entire project life into consideration.

Normally, the physical estimates for benefit and recurring cost are formulated for the entire life period of the project. The physical yields and the resources utilised are valued in terms of either the prevailing market prices or some accounting prices reflecting the real value of the output and the input to the society at the point of time referred to, where market mechanism is in operation. Otherwise, an imputed value may have to be adopted. In fact the net return estimate should reflect society's valuation of benefit yielded from the project. Benefit results from the operation of the project. Hence in order to study the impact of the project, two hypothetical conditions are to be borne in mind. A situation that is likely to prevail at a particular point of time without the project being executed. Another, that is expected to prevail on completion of the project. The change in the value of selected indicators as a consequence of the execution of the project is the measure of benefit or return. In technical term this is denoted as with and without principle. Since accurate estimates for hypothetical situation are difficult to be made, for all practical purposes the two situations, the one prevailing before the initiation of the project and the other after its completion, are compared. So it is easier to apply the criterion in post execution stage when 'before and after' conditions can be explicity recorded. Normally, however, the present position is compared to a projected value for the future, where probably environmental changes are neglected. This is an approximation to before and after method. The with and without principle is more scientific, though the second one can be more easily adopted to a particular situation.

Estimation of Benefit

This apparently easy technique however is not easily applicable in practical sphere because a number of nicetics are involved. How to arrive at an exact measure of social benefit to be derived from a project? How to choose economic life period of the project? What should be the rate of discount? Are the proceeds from the project to be reinvested? If so, where will the reinvestment take place? All these issues are to be clarified at the outset in order that the criterion may be suitably applied. The first problem relates to estimation of benefit. The method normally presupposes the possibility of quantitative assessment of the flow of returns from investment. Technique of assessment may vary from case to case. Sometimes returns can be ontained simply by valuing output at market prices. Sometimes, market prices may have to be modified, while at other times returns are to be deduced by analysing the nature of investment.

Type of Benefit : Benefits are broadly divided into two categories, e.g., tangibles (those which can be measured uniformly) and intangibles (those which cannot be measured uniformly). Tangible benefits again admit of two sub-classes-direct and indirect. Direct benefit is the sum total of the value of immediate products and services resulting from the measures for which project costs are incurred; indirect benefits are all other benefits that can be associated with the project somehow or other. For example, improvement of a road increases the mobility of commodities and men. Reduction in the cost of mobility, saving in travel time etc. are all instances of direct benefit. Now, traffic facilities are expected to increase market potential. As a result, production of commerial crop may be encouraged. This is of the nature of indirect benefit. For additional production will take place only when all other conditions are favourable and will not depend on road facility alone. Moreover, the existing facilities might have led to the introduction of the new crops sometime in future. The improvement of road in that case simply expedites the process. New roads quite often connect backward areas with progressive areas, thereby making possible cultural advancement of the former. Such benefit is clearly of intangible variety. While all the benefits are to be taken into consideration for analytical purpose, in formulating the quantitative criterion it is better to restrict the analysis to an estimation of direct benefit alone. Since a project does not bring about indirect benefit independently and intermediary as well as ancillary investment takes place, it is difficult to assign the share of a particular project in the final outcome. So there is always a danger of over estimation in case of indirect benefit. Intangible benefits do not admit of quantification.

Indicator of Benefit : The first step in benefit analysis is to choose suitable indicators of benefits. Other things remaining the same, a firm producing one single product for individual consumption offers no difficulty. The project return as also the social benefit to be derived is equivalent to sale proceeds, provided there is no serious market imperfection. But cost benefit technique is seldom applied in such cases. In the public sector where it is widely used, we come across projects which do not produce easily identifiable units of commodities or services, for example, free education, water supply, sanitary arrangement so forth and so on. Here, we have to choose an indicator that roughly corresponds to our idea of social benefit. We may take, total number of students completing a particular course or passing an examination as an indicator in the first case. Reduction in health hazards may be chosen in the other case.

Multiple return : A series of uses may flow from a single project. A typical case is that of a multipurpose river valley project. These are favourite public sector projects. The main objective of such a project is to provide irrigation facilities to increase agricultural output. But it also reduces the danger of flood. By storing water in dams it makes possible generation of electricity. Canals excavated for irrigational purpose are often navigable. They also provide facility for fishing. So all these benefits are to be taken into consideration and assessed separately. The sum total of benefits is to be incorporated in the final analysis.

Double counting and spill over effects : Just as not a single item of benefit is to be left out of account, double counting is to be carefully avoided. For that will lead to inflated figures covering fictitious benefit. Spillover effects are to be carefully segregated. Thus, in case of water transport the benefit is to be estimated either from the point of view of users of ferry services or from its organisers and not from both. The spillover effect is alternatively termed as external economics or diseconomics associated with a project. Thus when a new road is opened, some of the traffics of adjacent roads are diverted to it. When the purpose of construction of the road is to remove conjestion of other roads, the diversion of traffic is more beneficial than in a case where diversion leads to under utilisation of capacity of a neighbouring road.

Joint cost : Another difficulty arises when the ultimate effect is the resultant of a number of activities taken up simultaneously. For example, high yielding variety seeds may be introduced in a particular plot of land to increase output. The success of the programme depends to a large extent on provision of irrigational facilities, application of fertilisers and so on. So to associate the increase in output with the introduction of H.Y.V. seeds alone is an over simplification of the issue. Thus benefits which are exclusively due to a particular activity are to be carefully singled out. All improvements coming after the introduction of an activity should not be ascribed to that activity alone. Such wrong approach is often made in case of before after analysis. As for intangible benefits, if imputed values are reliable then they may be accepted. Otherwise, simple enumeration is better than any attempt at rough quantification.

Valuation of benefit : Once physical returns are thus estimated valuation problem occurs. In the first stage of measuring, i.e., in the estimate of physical returns, the unit of measurement is to be clearly defined so that price per unit can be easily assigned. Otherwise valuation becomes difficult at the very beginning. Next, for products that can be priced, the choice of price level in terms of which calculations are to be made is important. It is often suggested that in order to satisfy the purpose of benefit cost analysis, the prices that may reasonably be expected at the time of the benefit cost accrual would be accepted. But the practical difficulty in case of project appraisal is how to arrive at these expected price levels? In case of 'before and after' analysis, two separate prices referring to two different time periods should not be taken. The calculations may be made in terms of constant prices.

A second difficulty arises in respect of treatment of indirect taxes and subsidies. One view is to treat such taxes as benefits while the other view is to treat them as costs. The real point at issue is from whose point of view benefits are being considered. From the point of view of government, tax receipts are benefits and they are expected to increase as a result of the increase in people's ability to pay because of the operation of the project under consideration. If, however, the benefits are analysed from the point of views of individual beneficiaries, and that is how they should be looked upon, then the taxes are very clearly, costs and not benefits. So from the point of view of a particular project output may be valued at factor cost, i.e., market price (- indirect taxes + subsidies). All these discussions hold good when charging is possible. But there are instances of projects where charging is impossible. In such cases, values have to be imputed to the flow of benefit derived from a project.

Concept of Cost Including Labour Cost

Just as benefit in the sense of well-being of the people leads to abstraction, cost, in the sense of sacrifice involved does the same. Though such ideas are inherent in m.s.b. - m.s.c. criterion, they are not suitable for quantitative analysis. A given amount of resources may produce any one of a set of commodities. The opportunity cost of producing one particular item is the amount of other items forgone in the process of producing it. Thus if a government is to make a choice between two different types of projects say, a road project and an irrigation project — the opportunity cost of the first is the irrigational facilities sacrificed in the process and vice-versa. But in actual project planning a planner does not think so much of the opportunities forgone. He rather concentrates on deriving maximum advantage from the project that is to be lauched. He is therefore more interested in the amount actually spent. For all practical purposes therefore estimated or actual monetary cost is accepted with modifications here and there. For example, physical resources are valued at constant prices and wage cost adjusted to reflect the real sacrifice entailed by the society. Similarly when exchange control is in operation adjustments are made in respect of foreign exchange.

In the public sector, investment takes place mainly to provide the economy with a suitable capital structure, i.e., durable goods or fixed assets yielding a series of income. They involve relatively large amount of initial expenditure which normally spreads over a period of time and the length of time depends on the gestation period of production. Once the installation is complete, returns start flowing from it. But to realise the return, a recurring cost is to be incurred. Normally, returns begin to flow at a low ebb. Gradually it gathers momentum and reaches pick level when the capacity of the installation is fully utilised. Recurring cost may increase with the increase in the flow of return. But the capital or installation cost is determined once for all in relation to the productive capacity to be created. In the case of project appraisal, the justifiability of capital cost is mainly questioned. That is why, the returns are estimated net of recurring cost. Low initial investment may lead to the necessity of incurring huge maintenance and operating cost. Relatively large installation expenditure may involve considerable reduction in recurring cost. These will in their turn affect net return of the project.

In order to arrive at a measure of true economic cost, various refinements are introduced in cost concept. Normally economic cost differs from actual money cost when there is market imperfection and prices fail to reflect the real scarcity values of factors. This may happen when supply of the factor is in excess of demand or vice-versa. The case of excess supply is often manifested in labour market, specially in case of unskilled labour in underdeveloped economies. In the organised sector because of the prevalence of minimum wage laws and other regulations, some wages actually paid do not reflect the real costs of labour. When there is wide scale unemployment the opportunity cost of employing a group of unskilled labourers in a particular industry may be regarded as almost nil. When the economy is marked by extensive underemployment, the real costs of this type of labour is also much less than the actual wages paid. In underdeveloped economies, the primary sector is marked by acute underemployment. When unskilled labourers move from this sector to secondary or teritary sector, the opportunity cost in terms of output is not much. Still in view of the fact that labour shortage is experienced in peak seasons, the impact of withdrawal of unskilled labour on agricultural output should not be neglected altogether. But the real cost of unskilled labour in the organised sector will naturally be much less than the prevailing wage rate. For contribution of unskilled labour to agricultural output is much less than it is in industry in underdeveloped economies. Now in the primary sector, unskilled labourer normally consumes more than he produces. If real cost of labour is estimated from input requirements, level of consumption becomes important. The real cost of labour is often taken somewhere in between the two limits, inasmuch as a part of extra consumption over and above the marginal product of labour is counted as a disadvantage or cost. How far the level of consumption will come to the picture will depend on the society's attitude towards savings.

In case of skilled labour, interaction of supply and demand fixes the wage rate reflecting the economic cost to society. Sometimes the need for an exceptional type of skill in the economy may be very great and the wage rate may be lower than the real cost of this type of labour to the society. But such cases account for a negligible portion of total wage bill. Even if no adjustments are made on such accounts it will not make difference to project choice. For all practical purposes it is better to leave aside skilled labour on the assumption that here wages more or less reflects the true economic cost to society. Cost in respect of unskilled labourers which normally constitutes the bulk of labour cost (specially in construction work) has to be revised downwards, indicating the lower real cost of labour to society. The rate of deduction will depend on the marginal productivity of labour in the primary sector on the one hand and the level of consumption expenditure on the other.

Rate of Discount

Next, in the case of investible funds the economic return on the alternative uses should be taken as the price of capital and this may not be equal to market rate of interest. In practical sphere different rates of interest are charged for different types of capital fund by different lending authorities. Choice of a unique rate of discount is a complicated issue. Theoretically, two types of rates are referred to in economic discussions for analytical purposes -- the social time preference (S.T.P.) rate and the social opportunity cost (S.O.C.) rate. S.T.P. rate is expected to reflect societies' valuation of the relative desirability of consumption at different points of time. This will be different from individual time preference rate, since the society as a whole is likely to put a higher premium on future benefit. The S.O.C. rate is a measure of return to society from the next best alternative in which funds employed in the public sector project might otherwise have been used. It reflects the marginal productivity of capital. Since perfect competition is to be found nowhere in reality, no single rate of interest can accurately measure the social opportunity cost of fund.

In traditional capital theory a single rate of interest is determined at the point of equality between marginal time preference of savers and the marginal productivity of capital in investment. But in real world, in a mixed economy with market imperfections and multiple interest rates no single discount rate can be taken as a measure of both time preference and the productivity of capital. Moreover, even if there exists a perfect capital market, the rate of interest reflecting individual's time preference would be unsuitable for evaluating public sector projects. However, economists using cost benefit technique for project appraisal in public sector, are in search of a single discount rate, with normative significance for public expenditure decision. They are of the opinion that one or more than one rate may be decided upon by central authority for using in all project analysis. The rate may be called the accounting rate of interest or in short, A.R.I. These rates are to be settled by considering the overall economic position of a country, e.g., the demand for investible funds and the funds actually at the disposal of the society, the balance of payment situation, the level of wages so forth and so on. The A.R.I. will change with changes in economic environment. But for a limited period of time it is perhaps worthwhile to treat the rate as constant.

Since A.R.I. depends on economic environment, its value differs from country to country depending on the stage of development to which each belongs. According to Little & Mirrles[1] in a fairly advanced country the A.R.I. is not likely to be lower than 10 p.c. It may go up to 15 p.c. in some cases. Underdeveloped countries having relatively inefficient economic structure may fix the rate at 6 to 7 p.c. But under no circumstances should it be lower than 5 p.c. In their own language .... "It would seldom be worth going below 5 p.c. since returns of that order (after allowing for inflation, can be earned) with reasonable security in the international capital markets to which any country has access". Sometimes, costs and benefits may be discounted at different rates of interest high, low and medium. In a more or less controlled economy, the long term government interest rate may be expected to represent S.T.P. rate to a certain extent. It also partly represents the opportunity cost of diverting investible fund from private sector. A public sector project expected to enjoy a long life period may accept this rate as a rate of discounting in the absence of a more reliable one. A premium may be added for uncertainty. The outcome of a project not yet undertaken can merely be guessed. The future performance of an installation cannot be guaranteed even by an expert technician. The longer the view that we take the greater will be the uncertainty, specially in underdeveloped economy.

External Trade

In an open economy, measurement of benefit and cost poses further problem. To be fair, output and input should be valued at world prices. Whether the unit of account be home currency or foreign currency, the point at issue is that the scarcity value of foreign currency should be properly weighed. Not all currencies are to be placed on the same footing with regard to their scarcity values. Not only that, values themselves change through time. But when resources are utilised by importing them from abroad their cost to the society may actually be greater than what it would have been otherwise. Similarly, import content of a certain category of output is to be analysed carefully. Otherwise we shall fail to form a clear idea about their exact role.

In an economy only a handful of items are actually exported and list of import is never too large. But most of the outputs may be exported or used as import substitutes. Broadly, goods may be divided into two categories — traded and non-traded. In the first group those which directly enter into foreign trade or are capable of playing some sort of influence on it may be included. Foreign exchange involvement of this category can be more easily ascertained. In the other case also where output do not impinge on foreign exchange earning or spending so much, the foreign exchange component of its input contents is to be ascertained and corrections are to be introduced accordingly. This is more urgent in case of underdeveloped economy where foreign exchange is scarce.

Developing countries like India normally take recourse to exchange control in order to conserve and effectively utilise their limited earnings of foreign exchange. On account of such control the internal price of foreign currency does not reflect its actual scarcity value to society. The real cost of the project requiring foreign exchange for the import of machinery etc., should be calculated reflecting the scarcity value of the foreign exchange. If the project itself is one which has immense potentiality for saving import, suitable adjustments on account of foreign exchange is a must for guiding the selection process. The import saving potential of a project like ordinary rural road is not much. In fact road service is a non-traded item. But it may require imported inputs. Therefore some adjustments are necessary in the project cost. First the share of imported input is to be ascertained and then that portion is to be valued at its real cost to the society.

Time Period

Now once benefit estimates and cost items are suitably adjusted to arrive at a fair measure of social cost and social benefit these two items are compared to assess the social gain arising out of a project. Every investment has a gestation period - large or small. And return starts flowing only when the project is completed. Moreover in order to keep the flow of return unimpaired a recurring cost is to be incurred. Hence benefit and cost streams do not relate to a particular point of time, rather they occur at different points of time. To be precise the entire flow of benefit and cost throughout the life period of the project is to be taken into consideration for arriving at a proper choice of project. Benefits and costs are however compared at a particular point of time, may be at the time of initiating the project. Each item is therefore to be discounted back to this point taking into consideration the length of project life.

The estimation of actual life period of a project can never be precise in most cases. It is mostly a subjective process depending on the assessments of the physical length of life, technological changes, shifts in demand, etc. Capital asset normally wears out in course of time or becomes obsolete and will have to be replaced after a certain period of time. The life period is different for different types of assets. For example, in case of a machine or a transport equipment the life period is more or less technologically determined and a salvage value may be attributed to the asset when it is fully used up. But the problem is not the same for an irrigation project (like construction of a dam) or a road project.

Apparently these projects do not fall into the category of capital assets that have a limited life, they are not likely to 'wear out' if properly maintained. So they may be regarded as perpetual assets. But whatever is true about their technical life, will not hold for economic life. For example, if traffic along a road through a developing area goes on increasing and the road becomes too congested, up grading will be necessary thereby marking an end to the economic life of the previous road. In fact there is little point in taking an unusually long period into consideration while selecting a project, though there are enthusiasts who carry out their analysis for a time horizon of even 100 years. But there seems to be very little significance of such an elaboration. Economic environment as well as economic needs are bound to change with the passage of time. Hence, the measure of benefit may not remain the same. For example, in case of road, reduction in vehicle operation cost may be high at the initial stage while it may become negligible with the increase in traffic density in course of time. Moreover, the longer the period the smaller will be the significance of discounted values of benefit towards the end of the series. Then again there is no point in holding a discount rate to be constant for a long period. Hence the project analysis normally takes a limited horizon say, 50 to 60 years for irrigation projects and 30 to 40 years for road projects. The longer life period for irrigational project suggests that its economic impact is less susceptible to changes through time.

Role of Uncertainty and Sensitivity Analysis

Generally cost benefit analysis is undertaken in terms of a single estimate of benefit and a single estimate of cost. Similarly, unique values are also assigned to parameters like rate of discount, life period of the project etc. But in real world economic events do not occur with regularity. For example, traffic forecasting based on past traffic data and environmental studies may not come true due to some unforseen circumstances. It is a common experience that cost estimates at the time of project preparation often falls far short of the actual cost of construction, even if there are no significant changes in input prices. In various project formulations, there is a certain contingency allowance to guard against unforeseen circumstances. Still the gap between estimated and actual cost is not bridged. The scope for taking precaution is further limited in case of benefit or return estimates. Economic events often depend on factors beyond the control of a project analyst.

The elements of risk and uncertainty are being gradually incorporated in cost benefit analysis now-a-days. The future outcome of a project is uncertain for two obvious reasons. The data on which the analysis is based may not be fully reliable. Portions of the conglomaration may at best be rough approximation to reality. The effect of uncertainty is transmitted to the projections of benefit cost estimates. Secondly, these estimates range through time. And future itself is uncertain. The longer is the time period covered, the greater is the uncertainty involved. But such exercises should not be left aside on that ground.

In fact certain steps have already been suggested to face the difficulty. The traditional approach consists in advocating adoption of conservative values of benefit estimate. The sum total of discounted value of benefit is relevant for the calculation of N.P.V. or benefit cost ratio. Since the riskiness increases with passage of time it also advocates inclusion of a risk primium in the rate of discount. Shorter project life is another safeguard which may be taken recourse to. A more sophisticated approach is to incorporate probability analysis into the system. Instead of relying on a single 'best' value it is better to take into consideration a range of alternatives. The analysis consists in aggregating the probability judgements about many basic variables and parameters affecting the final outcome of a project into an estimate of the probability distribution of the final outcome. The calculations are elaborate, but mechanical devices have been sufficiently developed now a days to tackle the issue. In spite of a high degree of sophistication it is not free from subjective elements just as the other ones.

In order to account for uncertainty, at present sensitivity analysis is being developed systematically. The calculation of cost/benefit ratios, NPV or IRR depends on a number of variables. Some of them (e.g. shadow price of foreign exchange, social rate of discount) are exogeneously determined by a central authority. Some of them depend on technological considerations, e.g., life period of the project, reinvestment component. Sensitivity analysis consists in estimating different values of the final measure by changing the values of project variables and thereby finding out the sensitivity of the ultimate measure to different values of the variables. For example, a number of probable values of parameters like shadow exchange rate, discount rate etc. may be taken to get different sets of values of the ratio or the NPV. If within a certain range of values, the project responds favourably the project analyst will be in a better position to recommend the project. A single measure may be laden with imperfections. But a set of alternative values are likely to assist the decision making process better. The larger the number of variables incorporated in sensitivity analysis the more numerous will be the values of final measure. The discussions held so far prepare a general background for applying cost benefit analysis for project appraisal. Actual application will to some extent depend on physical environment and such other characteristics of the project.

Benefit Analysis in the Transport Sector

With this theoretical background in mind we now concentrate on the issue of applicability of the criterion to transport projects. Railways, airways and waterways are fortunate in as much as they carry a uniform traffic. Therefore variation in indicator of benefit is not wide. But the case of road project is different. Roads may be of various designs and specifications depending on the characteristics of the area that they are going to serve. Accordingly, indicators of benefits to be associated with different projects are not same everywhere. The purpose of a road is to provide connection between two habitation points. A narrow muddy track may serve the purpose in an interior village. But as soon as a pucca road is built connecting the village with a neighbouring town, the impact is felt throughout the entire village. Since the former is some sort of a free gift of nature nobody is interested in the assessment of benefit in its case. The second facility, however, is not likely to pass unnoticed. The effects of a multi-lane, bituminous modern highway having limited accessibility and with complete separation of grades may be more numerous. Hence, it may need a separate treatment altogether.

There is no denying the fact that the main direct benefit of a new construction or an improvement of a road accrues to the traffic that it bears. The composition of traffic, however, is not the same everywhere. It changes with the change in the specification of road, or in other words, the standard of a road is devised in accordance with the traffic pattern that it expects to bear. All roads are sure to give access to pedestrians. Of course, none has attempted to assess the satisfaction of a pedestrian moving along a road as also the change in the level of satisfaction with the improvement on the road surface. It is the movement of vehicular traffic in which evaluators are interested. These vehicles may be slow moving or fast moving. An improvement in road may replace the former by the latter or it may increase the speed of the former type. Thus the indicator is to be selected by studying actual conditions. In developed economies, motor vehicles are in wide use. Improvement of road is often regarded as a direct cause of the discovery of improved method of road transport. Hence, a list of indicators associated with the movement of motor vehicles are normally accepted as standard measures of benefit. These are increase in speed, safety consideration, comfortable travel and reduction in operation cost. These indicators can also be accepted for other modes of transport. All these benefits are sought to be measured quantitatively.

Saving in time : Improved road conditions increase vehicular speed. Slow moving animal driven vehicles are replaced by fast moving motor driven vehicles. Smooth surfaces of pucca roads also make possible faster movement. In fact all improvement in modes of transport take place with a view to ensuring speed.

People thus save travel time. Hence benefit is measured in terms of time saved by the occupier of the vehicles during their journey. But the valuation of time differs from person to person. One man may have to perform the journey to reach his place of work, while, to another it may simply be a pleasure trip. In one case the work may be urgent and any delay may involve some monetary loss. In another case, the urgency may not be there at all. Then, old men, children, i.e., people belonging to non-working group also travel. Valuation of time is not possible in such cases. Normally since saving in travel time due to increased speed can be assessed given adequate traffic data, value of time is sought to be deduced in different ways. Per capita income for the people of the region is often made use of. If a choice exists between a toll road and ordinary road to reach a single destination, where the former makes possible speedier movement then the toll rate may also be accepted as value of time saved by those moving along the road. In case of commercial vehicles, carrying goods, value of time saved by the driver may be deduced from his wages. This is likely to be quite accurate if he is paid at a piece rate, and he is free to utilise his time in any way he likes. Again if a person prefers air travel to travel by rail or road the difference in fares paid may measure his value of time. Thus, value of time is differently assessed and a single measure is adopted for a particular project. In order to make the overall picture reliable, a distinction between working class and non-working class within the passenger traffic can also be made. But, while collecting data, such subtle distinction is difficult to be enforced.

Reduction in accident : Increase in safety level is just another name for reduction in accident. An accident involves temporary loss of working capacity, damage or loss of commodities and sometimes loss of life. A monetary measure in the first two cases can be obtained. Loss of income during convalescent period and cost of treatment for full recovery may be regarded as monetary loss sustained as a result of the accident. So reduction in incidence of accidents will entail avoidence of monetary loss of this form. In the case of commodities (mainly vehicles) replacement and repair costs may also be taken into consideration. But the third item 'loss of life' does not admit of such generalised form of valuation, though life saving may be the greatest benefit to be derived from increase in safety level. Safely consideration plays an important role in all transport arrangement.

Comfort and pleasure of journey : Improvement of roads also makes the journey comfortable. Congestion is reduced, there is no jerking. But the mental satisfaction or physical comfort derived from smooth, uninterrupted journey is not amenable to physical measurement. Therefore, this category may rightly be placed under the heading — intangible benefit. Some indications may be available in car owner's preference for toll roads. In case of other modes of transport like railways, waterways extra charges are made for provision of extra comfort. Value of comfort may be deduced from their fare structure. But the idea is rather far-fetched.

Reduction in vehicle operation cost : Reduction in vehicle operation cost is the most important form of direct tangible benefit to be derived from all major transport projects and specially from the development of road communication. In a developed economy where motor vehicles are the most important type of road transport and road standards are maintained at a fairly high level, this item gets maximum attention. With the improvement of road surface, loss due to wear and tear of tyre diminishes. Fuel costs, lubricant costs too come down. There is a decrease in consumption of spare parts. Moreover, owing to smooth and unhampered flow of traffic,-the vehicle is better utilised. Hence, with the same level of fixed costs in the form of vehicle tax, salaries of operational staff etc. better level of service is enjoyed. But proper valuation of reduction in vehicle operation cost requires collection of extensive data on volume and composition of traffic. Operation costs are different for different types of vehicles and under different surface conditions. Hence reduction in operation cost is to be separately calculated for each type of vehicle under each circumstance. Values thus obtained are to be multiplied by the corresponding number of a particular vehicle using the road. Reduction in cost may take place in another way, which is quite apparent when a new alignment is opened to remove congestion in an existing alignment, often reducing the distance between two points in the process. Since, the distance is smaller and the new route is less congested, fewer vehicles or fewer trips may be necessary to carry the same number of passengers or the same amount of commodities between two termini. Consequently, there will be saving in the total cost of transportation. Improvement of road surface may also introduce fast moving vehicles in place of slow moving ones thereby reducing unit cost of journey.

The crucial factor in cost benefit analysis is to hit upon right choice of indicators of benefit and their proper quantification. The rest of the analysis follow a more or less standard pattern. While the indicators discussed in the previous section are suitable for transport projects in general, not all of them can be universally accepted. For example, some of these indicators may be suitable for assessing benefit of high-grade arterials while more restrictions may be needed for short distance rural road. Moreover, all these indicators relate to direct benefit while road improvement may exert a more potent indirect benefit by way of reorganising the entire economy. The case study that has been presented in the next section concentrate on direct benefit alone.

REFERENCES

1. M.D. Little & G.M. Mirrles - Manual of Industrial Project Analysis in Developing Countries, Vol. II, O.E.C.D.

2

AN EXERCISE IN APPLICATION

Introduction

From the previous discussions it is clear that the cost benefit analysis is a quantitative technique which seeks to test prospective or actual performance of a project objectively. Practical application of the criterion can hardly fulfil the ideal conditions laid down in theoretical analysis. The criterion is applied here in the post execution stage of a road project. The analysis has taken recourse to abstractions and generalisations since data cannot be collected under ideal conditions. This case study refers to a point of time in mid sixties when the project was completed. The traffic and catchment areas surveys which supplied the basis for benefit estimate were taken up around that time. Since it is simply an exercise in application of the theoretical framework built up in the previous chapter, the time period is not of much significance. The exposition shows how the criterion is to be applied at a particular point of time, how to analyse direct benefit of a rural road and how to quantify the benefit. It also illustrates how to convert monetary cost and benefit into social cost and benefit.

Whenever a new road is built or an old one improved, two sets of people enjoy the benefits. First, those who live by the road side feel its impact. Secondly, those who pass along the road enjoy certain additional advantage. Every improvement in road yields some direct vehicular benefit. On the whole it ensures smooth running of existing volume of traffic and attracts new traffic also. The new road, by ensuring greater mobility, ushers in far reaching economic consequences. Improved roads are likely to induce new investments which bring about reorganisation of land use and strategic rearrangement of industrial plants, mercantile establishments, social services and residences,

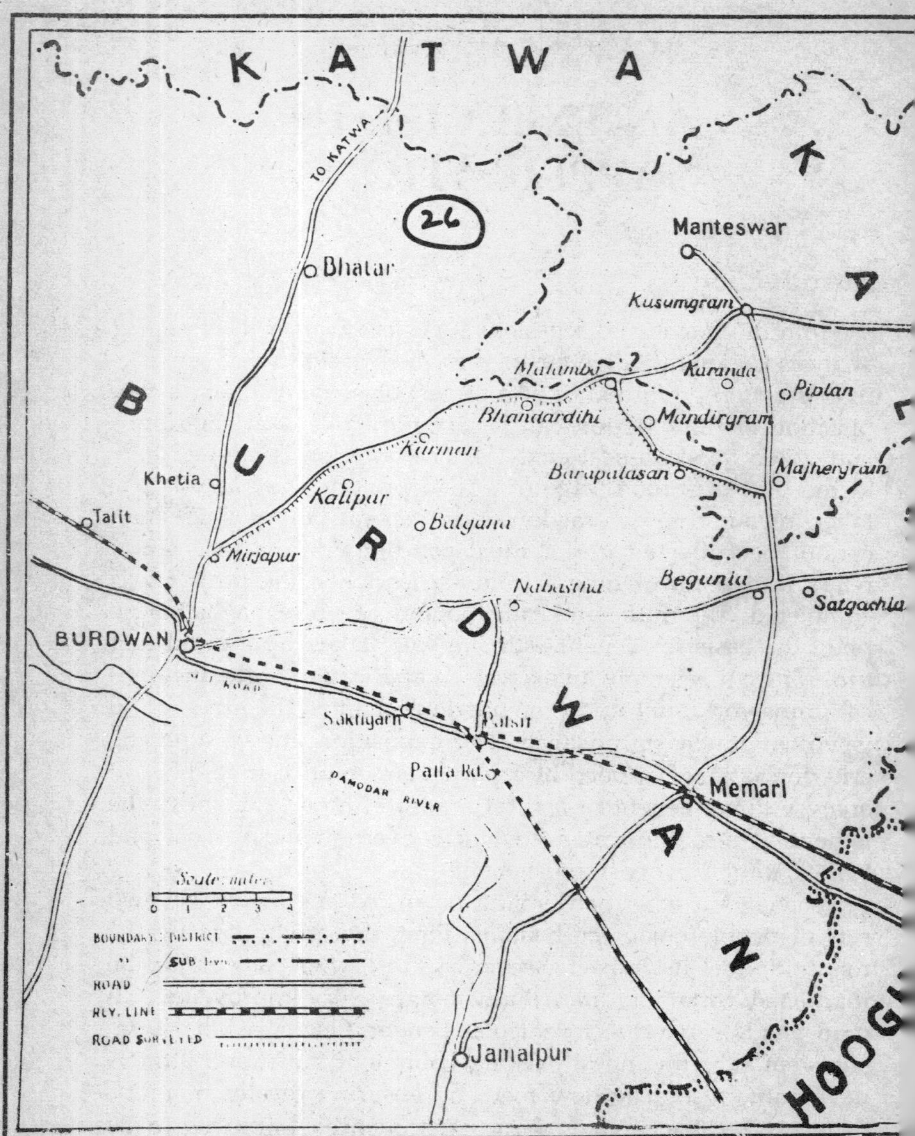

Road Map of M.K.M.M. Road in Burdwan District

with respect to the road network. However, if benefits are sought to be thus elaborated, we do not know where to stop. Therefore indicators will have to be chosen carefully depending on the types of services rendered. Since direct vehicular benefit is least controversial, we concentrate on this benefit alone to avoid dangers of over estimation and wrong estimation to a considerable extent.

The Road and its Catchment Area

The road section selected in the study is locally called the Mirjapur-Kaligram-Malamba-Majergram road. It is located in Burdwan district of West Bengal. There was a discontinuity after Majergram due to land acquisition problem in the sixties. This was subsequently resolved and the potentialities of the road section have further increased. We however stick to the position as it stood at the time of completion of M.K.M.M. road towards the end of sixties. It is an arterial providing interconnection between a prosperous paddy growing area (paddy being the main food crop of West Bengal) to the agricultural markets of Burdwan. As a result of the opening of this road, the villages in the catchment area were connected with two important agricultural markets—Burdwan and Memari — Burdwan being much nearer to the area. The total length of the road was 22 miles and 47 chains or roughly 36.84 Km. Originally it had been a kucha road, narrow, tortuous and full of local depressions. Because of the depressions the road would become unusable with a slight rainfall. In fact it used to remain unsuitable for any kind of traffic for most part of the year. The imporved road mostly followed the old alignment. The width of the improved road came to be 10′ (black topped portion) with 5′ flanks on either side. The thickness of the road was 1′3″. The alignment passed mainly through flat, open, non-flooded area with uneven land at some places. The soil was mainly sandy clay. The total cost of construction was Rs. 20,30,000 and annual maintenance cost came to a little over Rs. 1 lakh in the sixties.

The improved road came under the category of 'other district road' (O.D.R.) i.e. a rural road providing interconnection within a particular locality and not a trunk road passing beside important administrative and commercial towns while covering vast tracts of rural areas on the way. Nevertheless, this was not a typical land access road. It was an arterial connecting a patch of rural area with the administrative headquarter and marketing centres. Instead of running in between villages it ran through the outskirts of small habitations. But the road used to have local importance only. The standard of construction reveals that it was not expected to carry heavy traffic so much. The improvement, however, introduced a change in the composition of traffic which was extremely significant for the area.

The road was officially declared complete sometime in December, 1965 and was thrown open to traffic near about that time. According to the people of the locality, the area had undergone a complete transformation as a result of this improvement. The economy was reorganised so to say, and one could easily feel the beneficial effect on the standard of living of the people. People in general, were in a position to earn more because of better marketing facility and greater availability of quality input.

In order to form an idea about the nature and extent of reorganisation of the catchment area, a sample survey of villages was conducted in March, 1969 before the final traffic survey. The area map shows that there are as many as ninetyone villages lying within a radius of five miles from this road on either side. Not all of them appeared to be depending on this road exclusively, since some other important major district roads like Burdwan-Kalna and Memari-Manteswar roads also lie quite close to the area. From this framework, twenty villages were selected at random. Of these sampled units, the inhabitants of eight villages depended on this road as their only means of communication. The villagers in the other twelve villages, could make use of some other roads also. Normally, four to six old residents of these villages were approached with questionnaires. These knowledgeable persons like Anchal Pradhans, school teachers, grocers, cart manufacturers and such other persons supplied valuable information regarding the conditions of the economy before and after the improvement of the road. Being old residents they were expected to bear testimony to the change.

The enquiries in the villages revealed that the area did not have any railway or any waterway as an alternative to road way. So this pucca road exerted a tremendous influence on the area. Prior to the improvement, the entire area was completely isolated from the rest of the district. The area being a part of eastern Burdwan was fertile, with agricultural potential, but extremely backward at that time. Not a single brick-building could be found in the area. Agriculture was the main occupation. Apart from agriculture, the only other trade was to build bullock-carts, those being the sole means of transport at that time. A handful of people were engaged in it. Interestingly enough, most of them had migrated to this place from some other region; local people were all attached to land and no other occupation of any significance could be found in the area. Traffic had been too small, the main purpose of travel being marketing. A few local shops used to supply daily necessities to the local people. Because of transport difficulties and low volume of sale, only few commodities used to be brought in small quantities by the traders. The demand profile had not been encouraging. People had little purchasing power, the income being derived mostly from the sale of paddy. The wage rate had been low. The peasants were exploited by middle men since they were not familiar with market conditions and crop prices due to communication difficulties.

The only other salable product of some significance had been dairy product because of concentration of traditional milkman families in certain villages. Even these products failed to fetch good price since they were not to be exported in bulk to nearest urban centres due to poor communication. The idea appears to be quite justified when we find that condition of the village Rayan connected by a pucca road with Burdwan was not at all backward all these days. It was enjoying a prosperous existence for a pretty long time.

The villagers when interviewed, also gave their impression about the catchment area after the improvement of M.K.M.M. road. Production was diversified to some extent. Though paddy remained the principal crop villagers took recourse to cultivation of wheat, potato, surgarcane, etc. Milk product, mainly casein came to be exported in bulk to the sweetshops at

Burdwan. Certain ancillaries to agriculture operation like bone mills, husking mills sprung up in road side villages.

A rise in standard of living was perceptible as new products like soap, tea, biscuits entered consumer budget. The most important items appeared to be coal and kerosene. The villagers changed their fuel habits from cowdung, wood lot to more sophisticated form. The figures supplied by grocery shops in a road side village Kurmun revealed that sale of kerosene and oilcakes had increased fifteen times and five times respectively in five years. The appearance of masonary structures, specially on road side villages, was another encouraging sight.

Though villagers retained bullock carts for carrying commodities as also visiting, urban centre, bicycles became a favourite vehicle. Groceries began to bring goods in bulk in trucks. The introduction of bus service brought the final stroke. People came into contact with educational, recreational and health facilities of urban centres and slowly it began to introduce a cultural transformation.

But whatever be the underlying impetus behind these changes, it is illogical to attribute the expansion entirely to road development. Part of the impetus might have come from factors other than road development. For example, diversification in production in the agricultural sector was really due to intensive development programmes in the sphere of irrigation, fertiliser etc. undertaken in the district as a whole. Again, tea and coal perhaps entered consumption budget of villagers because of changing environment. Nobody can exactly associate a fixed percentage share of increase in total sale of consumption goods with the investment in road. One point however is evident from all these discussions that since the improvement of the road, export from and import to the region increased. This is also borne out by the results of two commodity movement surveys undertaken before and after the improvement of the road. The extent of reduction in transport cost and increased volume of commodity-flow are unquestionably indicators of benefit that can be ascribed to investment in road. Similarly, benefit arising out of greater mobility of people living in the region is also a significant benefit to be counted upon. Hence our quantitative analysis is restricted to vehicular benefits only; it is not extended to other types of benefits which may be questioned.

Benefit Approach

In order to assess direct benefit enjoyed by road users a week-long traffic survey was conducted along the road in the last week of January 1970. So far as passenger traffic is concerned, the benefit estimates are based entirely on the results of the survey. But in case of commodity traffic comparison is made with the results of a previous survey. A detailed quintal mileage data was available with the Calcutta Metropolitan Organisation which had conducted a focal point survey at Dewandighi check-post (from 29th January to 4th February 1965) as a part of All India Regional Transport Survey. Our survey also accepted the focal point Dewandighi, since traffic corssed over to Burdwan from this point. The information gathered from village survey data is helpful for analysing traffic survey data in many ways.

In order to assess vehicular benefit first of all we have to start with traffic composition. As a consequence of the improvement on road, old traffic is likely to enjoy greater advantage. Traffic from alternative routes may be diverted with a view to enjoying special advantage. The improvement may induce altogether new traffic as well. In this case we find, benefit mainly accrues in the form of newly induced traffic. Since alternative transport routes had been nonexistent, there was no question of diversion of traffic. The old traffic consisted mainly of bullock carts. The benefit accruing to such a slow moving vehicle along an improved road is not of much significance. However it is taken into consideration in case of commodity traffic.

The direct benefits derived exclusively from improvement of the road can be systematically put in the following categories : (1) conveyance of passengers in bulk (in buses) or individually (in bicycles & motor cycles) or in small numbers (cars and rickshaws), (2) quick and less costly (in terms of unit transport cost) transport of raw materials, merchandise and food in fast moving motor vehicles (truck). These are to be converted into suitable measurable units. The following sections seek to present these benefits in quantitative term. Passenger traffic and commodity traffic are subjected to separate treatment. In case of commodity, traffic data prior to the improvement are available for a particular period. The position after the improvement is analysed against this background. For passenger benefit we start with the assumption that people moving along the road in vehicles would have travelled on foot had the road not been improved at all. Though bullock carts were used for passenger transport to some extent (mainly by vehicle owners), no indication was available regarding the volume of traffic prior to improvement.

The new road definitely increased the mobility of men and material. More and more goods came to be transported in lorries. The bullock carts could also move swiftly and smoothly. Now cost of operation of a vehicle along kucha road is higher than that in pucca road. Since fare charged is related to cost of operation, fare is normally higher along kucha road. In fact the benefit accruing to an improvement in road is the reduction in cost of operation in real terms e.g. reduction in fuel consumptions, increase in durability of tyres and tubes etc. These are converted into money terms. Measuring cost of operation is not so easy in case of bullock cart since it does not depend on mechanical devices but on strength and efficiency of animals. However, as movement along pucca road is easier in their case also, a lower fare is charged along pucca road. Hence reduction in fare is acceptable in this case. Thus reduction in cost of operation/fare is taken to be the indicator of benefit in case of commodity traffic. Though the immediate gain due to the reduction accrues to transport operator it is ultimately diffused among consumers. For it increases the scope of marketibility of product and reduces price disparity. As a commodity becomes easily available in wider area, competition among sellers brings down its price to a uniform level. The supplier includes transport cost within price. Hence prices are reduced in the areas served by improved road as a consequence of reduction in transport cost. Similarly other areas derive a price advantage in respect of exports from this region. The final gain is then transmitted to consumers and this is intercepted of the first stage as reduction in cost of operation/fare of vehicle in this study.

In case of passenger traffic fast moving vehicles of different types were introduced along the road after the improvement.

Moreover, their services were being utilised by people belonging to different income groups. Increased speed made possible better utilisation of manpower. By saving journey time, additional working hours were released. Hence this improvement is likely to have an impact on productivity. Nevertheless, we cannot logically conclude that a fixed part of the increase in production in the adjoining area was entirely due to the increase in working hours. Rather we may view the situation from the standpoint of an individual. Now a passenger gains some extra time by covering a certain distance in a vechicle rather than travelling on foot. He is expected to utilise this extra time in some work yielding an income to him. This is his gain from saving in time. But he incurs a cost by travelling in vehicle. Hence his net hourly gain is the difference between hourly income and hourly cost. This is accepted as the indicator of benefit. Thus in both cases the underlying idea is to hit upon some sort of consumers' surplus enjoyed by individuals as a consequence of the improvement. But certain simplification have been introduced in quantitative analysis due to paucity of data.

Commodity Traffic and Cost of Vehicle Operation

The benefit estimate is made for the year 1970 when a week-long traffic survey was undertaken. The road capacity came to be more or less fully utilised at that time. The period covered in the survey ranges from 25.1.70 to 31.1.70. The checkpoint was located at Dewandighi — the starting point of the road from Burdwan-Katwa road. There are two reasons for selecting this particular point. Traffic originating and terminating at Burdwan normally pass through this point. Since Burdwan is the nearest town and market place of this area most of the traffic normally move in between Burdwan and this region. Secondly, in January-February 1965, almost a year before the completion of the road, a week-long commodity movement survey had been undertaken along Burdwan-Katwa road by the Calcutta Metropolitan Planning Organisation at the same check post under the auspices of Joint Technical Group for Transport Planning. This survey had intercepted the traffic of the catchment area of M.K.M.M. road, as is evident from the name of several origin and destination points in the schedules. On the strength of the data collected in that survey the weekly volume of commodity movement on different vehicles prior to the upgrading of the road are obtained. These consolidated figures give us an idea of the condition prevailing prior to the improvement of the road. The survey conducted by us brings to light the post development picture. To start with, the results of the survey undertaken in 1970 are analysed. An interesting feature revealed in this survey is that long distance traffic were scarcely seen along this road. Vehicles normally originated and terminated somewhere along the strech, Majergram-Burdwan. To the exclusion of carriers of coal, all other vehicles carrying commodities normally started from or finally stopped at Burdwan. The table 2.1 gives us an idea of composition of traffic along the road, as intercepted in our survey.

Table 2.1 : Utilisation of the Road*

S. No.	*Type of Vehicle*	*Weekly Volume of Traffic*			*Average Daily Volume of Traffic*
		To Burdwan	*From Burdwan*	*Total*	
1.	Cycle	1159	1039	2198	314
2.	Cart	591	621	1212	173
3.	Bus	217	217	434	62
4.	Lorry	126	125	251	36
5.	Rickshaw	80	60	140	20
6.	Scooter	35	41	76	11
7.	Jeep, Taxi	34	38	72	10
8.	Total	2242	2141	4383	626

*Weekly Traffic of Different Types of Vehicles Along the Road and Their Daily Averages

Source : Our Survey, 1970. Of these, carts and lorries are used almost exclusively for carrying commodities.

In case of commodity movement, we start with the result of C.M.P.O.'s survey held in 1965, just before the upgrading of the road. The weekly volume of commodity movement for the period was estimated to be 4399.95 qtl. of which imports came to 990.67 qtl. Export list contained three items mainly paddy, rice and straw. Food items like sugar, mustard oil, pulses etc. constituted total imports to the region. Regarding mode of transport, we find, carts to be the usual type. Motor vehicles were used for a limited distance. In fact 67 p.c. of the total volume of commodity was found to be carried in animal driven vehicles. Total quintal mileage, performed by the two types of vehicles was 38902.67 qt./m. Table 2.2 presents the results of the survey in a systematic form. It sums up the position prevailing before the improvement of road in respect of commodity movement.

Table 2.2 : Commodity Movement Along M.K.M.M. Road

		Export		*Import*		*Total*	
S. No.	*Type of Vehicle*	*Quantity in Qtl.*	*Qtl./m*	*Quantity in Qtl.*	*Qtl/m*	*Quantity in Qtl.*	*Qtl./m*
1.	Motor Vehicle	1065.00	11985.00	355.00	3645.50	1420.00	15631.00
2.	Animal Driven Vehicle	2344.28	18186.31	635.67	5085.36	2979.95	23271.67
3.	Total	3409.28	30171.81	990.67	8730.86	4399.95	38902.67

Source : C.M.P.O. Focal Point Survey in the Eastern Region.

Now, what was the position in 1970, 5 years after the completion of the road project. The timings of the second survey was kept more or less identical with the first to avoid seasonal variations. In quantitative term, figures show that both volume of commodity movement and qtl. mileages performed went up. Qualitatively major export items preserved the earlier pattern, while import list was diversified. Coal and building materials now became two major items, followed closely by fertiliser and kerosene. Table 2.3 sums up the results of the second survey.

Thus compared to the position in 1965, weekly volume of commodity movement went up from 4399.95 qtl. to 10606.80 qtl. i.e. by 141% while qtl. mileages covered, from 38902.67 qtl./m to

189666.50 qtl./m i.e. by nearly 5 times. Now, improvement in road, which facilitated smooth flow of commodities, is obviously responsible for this change. But for this improvement, it would not have been possible to carry commodities in bulk in motor vehicles. Moreover, improvement of the road surface reduced cost of operation. The reduced cost of operation for old traffic as also advantages derived from the new traffic are the two indicators of direct benefit.

Table 2.3 : Commodity Movement Along M.K.M.M. Road

S. No.	Type of Vehicle	*Export*		*Import*		*Total*	
		Quantity in Qtl.	*Qtl./m*	*Quantity in Qtl.*	*Qtl./m*	*Quantity in Qtl.*	*Qtl./m*
1.	Motor Vechicle	2937	64440	4272	98536	7209	162976
2.	Animal Driven Vehicle	1764.5	12943.3	1633.3	13747.2	3397.8	26690.5
3.	Total	4701.5	77383.3	5905.3	112283.2	10606.8	189666.5

Source : Our Survey, 1970.

The cost of operation per Km. of a truck of 8 tonnes/80 qtl. pay load is obtained from the Eastern Region Transport Survey Report 1968. Our traffic survey of 1970 revealed that the trucks plying along M.K.M.M. road were of this type. A U.N.O.[1] study on Transport categorically points out that cost of operation of a motor vehicle along a kucha road is normally 50 per cent higher than that along a metalled road. Now some items of the cost remain the same whatever be the type of road surface. In Table 2.4 the cost of operation data of a truck of 8 tonnes pay load along metalled surface as well as increase in cost along kucha road is presented. The difference in cost of operation on kucha road is estimated on the strength of the data published in a report in 1961.

In the Eastern Region Transport Survey depreciation cost is treated as a fixed cost too, while the other report has nothing to say about this cost. But it is roughly taken to be 20 per cent higher on kucha road in this study. The percentage increase of cost figures in respect of other items are taken from the second report, where instead of maintenance we get the item 'spare part.' The cost on this account is estimated to be higher by 200 per cent in kutcha road. We have taken maintenance cost to be a little higher (266 p.c.) because maintenance includes some thing more than expenditure on spares alone. Retaining the basic assumption of 50 per cent increase in overall cost, the extra amount is added to maintenance cost.

Table 2.4 : Cost of Operation Per Km. of a Truck of 8 Tonne Pay Load

		Cost of Operation Per Km. in Paise		
S. No.	*Items of Cost*	*Pucca Road*	*Per Cent Increase on Kutcha Road*	*Difference in Cost*
1.	Fuel & Oil	21.0	12%	2.5
2.	Tyres & Tubes	12.9	100%	12.9
3.	Maintenance	8.6	266%	23.6
4.	Depreciation Cost	13.2	20%	2.6
5.	Drivers T.A.	3.3	No Change	x
6.	Insurance, Taxes, Wages etc.	24.3	No Change	x
7.	Total	83.3		41.6

Source : 1) Eastern Region Transport Survey, 1968.
2) Report on road transport operation cost on various types of surfaces - Road Transport Operation Cost Committee, 1961.

Now, of all the different items of cost, fuel and oil, tyres and tubes, as also spare parts have import contents of varying amount. They have been assessed separately in order to make necessary adjustment on account of foreign exchange involvement. First of all estimates are made from the official data on all India consumption of fuel oil by vehicle category as also share of imported crude oil in total oil consumption by motor vehicles. The foreign exchange involvement is estimated to be 34 per cent for the year 1970. In case of tyres and tubes the percentage shares of foreign exchange are calculated to be 57.0, 11.3 and 6.2 in the year 1960, 1966 and 1970 respectively by manufacturing concerns.[2] From the consumption and the import figures for 'spare parts' in late sixties the import content is calculated to be 26.39 per cent.

In a developing country like India the scarcity value of foreign exchange is not relfected in its official price, which is a controlled price. Hence a premium is to be attached to the foreign exchange component and the rate of premium is to be decided. In the cost benefit studies undertaken by the Transport Research Wing (Ministry of Transport & Shipping) in sixties 50 per cent premium has been attached to foreign exchange component while deducing economic cost from monetary investment cost. In the clandestine market, the foreign exchange required to buy gold used to be acquired at a premium of about 70 to 80 p.c. in this country at that time. Hence, two other figures for saving in cost have been obtained by attaching 50 p.c. and 70 p.c. premium to foreign exchange.

Table 2.5 : Adjustment of the Difference in Cost of Operation in Respect of Foreign Exchange Component

S. No.	*Items*	*No Premium (Table 4 Col. 5)*	*Percentage Share of Foreign Exchange*	*50 Per cent Premium*	*70 Per cent Premuim*
1.	Fuel & Oil	2.5	34.00	2.92	3.09
2.	Tyres & Tubes	12.9	6.20	13.29	13.45
3.	Maintenance	23.6	26.39	26.71	27.95
4.	Depreciation	2.6	—	2.60	2.60
5.	Total (per truck km.)	41.6	—	45.52	47.09
6.	Total (per qtl./km.) Capacity 80 qtl.	0.52	—	0.57	0.59
7.	Total (per qtl./ml)	0.84	—	0.92	0.95

Therefore saving in qutl./ml in three cases come to .84 P., .92 P and .95 P respectively during sixties.

The advantage accruing to animal driven vehicle cannot however be estimated in terms of operation cost. But because of the inconveniences faced in earth road, cart drivers normally charged .50 P extra per mile in such roads in that region as was revealed in the village inquiries conducted during 1970. The capacity of a cart being 5.5 Qtl. the saving in fare per qtl./mile thus comes to $\frac{50}{5.5}$ P =9 P approximately. Thus while the gain is estimated from the point of view of actual cost incurred in the former case, it is taken to be the monetary saving of the user of vehicle service in the second case for lack of cost data. Now in order to estimate the benefit arising out of commodity traffic, the volumes are to be multiplied by respective cost saving figures and daily benefits are to be estimated taking into account the daily volume of commodity traffic.

The increase in daily commodity traffic is shown in Table 2.6.

Table 2.6 : Change in Daily Volume of Commodity Traffic After Improvement

S. No.	*Type of Vehicle*	*Volume of Commodity Movement*		
		Position in 1970 /qtl./mile	*Position in 1965 qtl./mile*	*Daily Increase qtl./mile*
1.	Motor Vehicle	23282.28	2233.00	21049.28
2.	Animal Driven Vehicle	3812.92	3324.52	488.40

[Derived form Table 2 & Table 3].

Comparing Table 2.2 and Table 2.3 we find weekly commodity flow as between 1965 and 1970 went up by 147345. 00 qtl./mile and 3418.83 qtl./mile under two vehicle categories, the corresponding daily figures being 21049.28 qtl./mile and 488.40 qtl./mile respectively (Table 2.6). The major portion of the increase in volume of commodity was being carried in motor vehicles. It appears from all accounts that increased flow of commodity may be due to at least three reasons — reduction in carrying cost which is also relfected in fare structure under competitive condition, rise in the level of demand and increase in road capacity. All these conditions were operating in M.K.M.M.

road. These three situations are treated separately in the following graphical illustrations.

Benefit Measured from Commodity Traffic

The supply curve (for transport services) is assumed to be infinitely elastic at the prevailing unit cost of operation/fare level in case of commodity traffic. Figure 2.1 depicts a case of reduction in transport cost. The supply curve has moved downwards. Commodity flow which was originally given by ST has come to S_1 M at the prevailing demand level due to cost reduction. The resulting benefit accruing to the users of vehicle services is given by the area enclosed by two supply curves and the demand curve. So far as the original amount of commodity flow is concerned the gain is measured by the area SR (ST.TR) i.e. the original volume of commodity flow X reduction in operation cost/fare. But for the extra amount RM, the gain is to be measured by the area TRM (1/2 RM.TR) i.e. 1/2 increase in commodity flow X reduction in cost/fare, approximately.

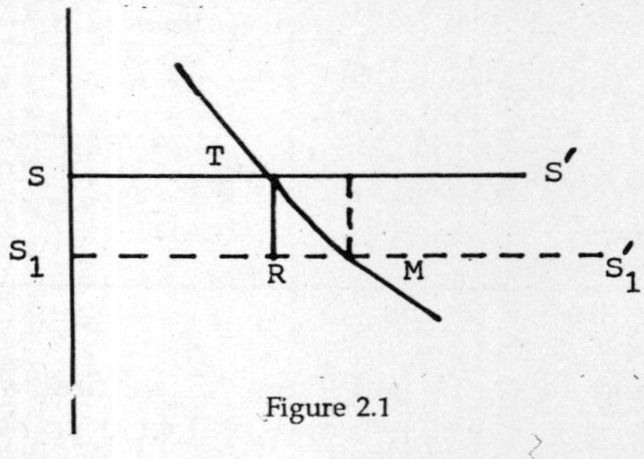

Figure 2.1

Figure 2.2 depicts a case of rise in demand for vehicle services. Let us suppose that because of the improvement of road, traffic movement has become easier and more convenient. Greater mobility leads to an increase in production as well as rise in living standard thereby expanding the volume of export from and import to the region. Hence demand for transport services for carrying commodities will rise also. If the demand curve $D_1D_1^1$ — depicts the new situation even without any cost reduction the extra gain accruing to the users of transport service will be given by DQ + T Q N. But quantitative assessment will not be possible in this case unless we have a clear knowledge of the demand functions.

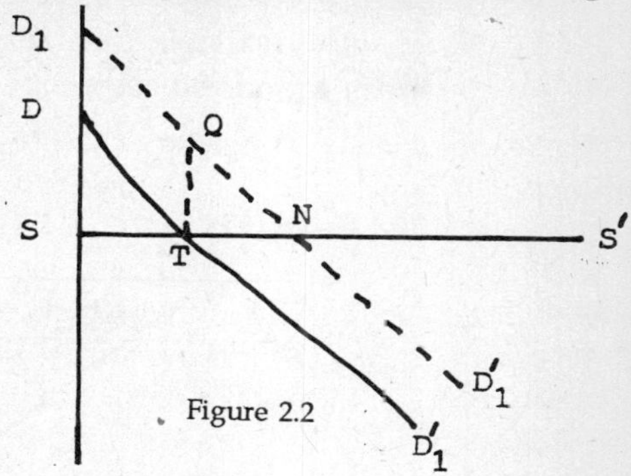

Figure 2.2

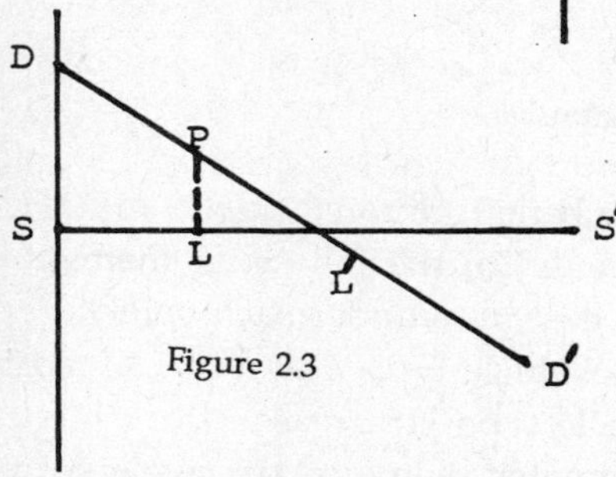

Figure 2.3

The commodity flow may have increased simply because the road can now carry more traffic i.e. the improvement has increased its capacity. Let us suppose that the original capacity of the road was limited to carrying SL amount of commodity in Figure 2.3. But, now as a result of the improvement the quantity carried is expanded to L'. The resulting benefit to the community presented by PLL' can hardly be measured unless the original and the new capacities and the demand function are definitely known.

Figure 2.4 represents a consolidated position combining all these three factors. The two points T and T_1 represent two hypothetical positions — say, the situations prevailing in 1965 and in 1970 respectively along M.K.M.M. road. In 1965, DD' and SS' represent demand and supply curves. Further let us suppose that in the year the capacity of the road is such that commodity flow cannot go beyond N. In 1970, the capacity has been expanded to a point say L, cost/fare reduction has taken place by an amount $S S_1$ and there is an upward shift of demand curve to D_1D_1' level. Clearly, overall benefit derived from the increase in commodity flow is represented by the following areas SR + TRM + TT_1 +T Q N + DQ. Of these only the first two areas can be measured with available data in this case study, while the rest of the areas cannot be ascertained.

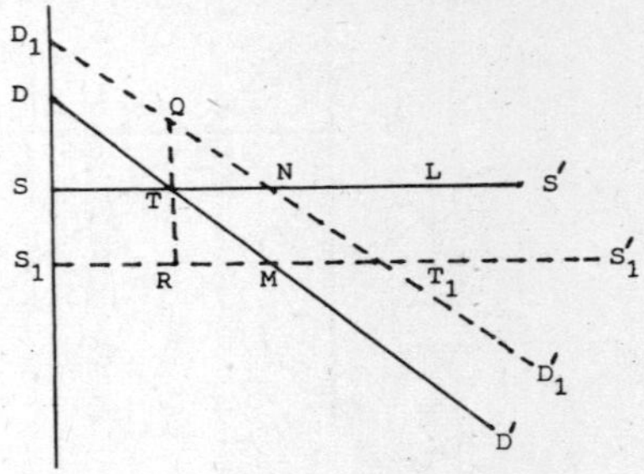

Figure 2.4

Hence, the commodity flow benefit derived due to reduction in transport cost/fare is estimated in the following manner — sum of reduction in transport cost/fare under each vehicle type x original commodity flow by vehicle type + sum of 1/2 reduction of transport cost by vehicle type x increase in commodity flow by vehicle type. The estimates therefore are conservative. Corresponding to different treatment of foreign exchange we get three estimates of benefit derived from motor vehicles. However we have a single estimate of daily benefit derived from animal driven vehicle. The benefit estimates for motor vehicles and animal drived vehicles are presented below.

These estimates relating to motor vehicles are based on 1965 price level, when the Eastern Region Survey was undertaken. In order to compare effectively cost and benefit estimates, the valuation unit of different items are to correspond to the same time period. In our case all the items have been valued at 1965 price level for reasons to be explained later on. Taking into account the wholesale price index of West Bengal in the two years 1965-66 and 1970-71 with 1952-53 as the base, a correction factor $\frac{159.2\ (1965)}{210.9\ (1970)} = .75$ is applied to each one of the item which are valued at 1970 prices. Since the fares in case of bullock cart have been

been obtained for the year 1970, the benefit estimate has been reduced to 1965 level to make it comparable to others.

Table 2.7 : Daily Benefit Estimate for Commodity Traffic at 1965 Prices

Type of Vehicle	*Original Commodity Flow*	*Increase in Commodity Flow*	*Savings in Operation Cost*	*Daily Benefit Estimate*
Motor Vehicle	2233.00 qtl./m	21049.28 qtl./m	No premium in F.E. 84 P.	Rs. 107.66
			50% " 92 P.	Rs. 117.37
			70% " 95 P.	Rs. 722.23
Animal driven	3324.52 qtl./m	480.40 qtl./mile	Saving in fare reduction 9 P. (in 1970)	Rs. 321.18
			Do (in 1965)	Rs. 240.88

(Derived from Tables 5 & 6).
N.B. The last row is obtained thus - Rs. 321.18 x .75 (correction factor) = 240.88.

Passenger Traffic

The earlier discussion noted that prior to the improvement of the road, passenger vehicles (to the exclusion of a few carts) seldom used the road. The passenger traffic data presented in Table 2.8 refers to a period after the improvement of the road. However, assuming the passenger miles covered in 1970 to be the same, with or without improvement, the possible gain in terms of saving in time enjoyed by the passengers has been accepted as an indicator of benefit. Since journey time for different vehicles as also the normal speed rate of a pedestrian are mostly known the saving in journey time is easily deduced and presented in the following section. But instead of taking all the vehicles we have singled out the first two only, for reasons to be explained later.

Assuming that, on an average, a healthy man can normally cover a distance of 3 miles per hour, time saved per mile by passengers of each vehicle category may be easily calculated. In case of buses, we find, uniform standard is being maintained

Table 2.8 : Daily Passenger Vehicle Traffic Along M.K.M.M. Road

S. No.	*Type of Vehicle*	*No. of Vechicle*	*Vehicle mile*	*No. of Passenger*	*Passenger Mile*
1.	Cycle	314	1289	336	1480
2.	Bus	62	1300	6627	52000
3.	Rickshaw	20	79	39	142
4.	Scooter	11	127	19	202
5.	Jeep, taxi	10	133	39	502
6.	Total	411	2928	7060	54326

Source : Our Survey, 1970.

by operators along the route. Each bus covered a distance of 20 miles in $1\frac{1}{2}$ h. Therefore the speed rate is 13.1/3 miles per hour approximately. The speed rate for bicycle is taken to be 7 miles per hour, which was averaged out of the information supplied by a few cyclists moving along the road. Daily passenger miles performed by each vehicle category were obtained from the results of the survey. The times saved in a day by passengers moving in buses and cycles are estimated and presented in Table 2.9.

Table 2.9 : Time Saved Per Day by Bus Passengers and Cyclists

S. No.	*Item of Information*	*Type of Vehicles*	
		Bus	*Cycle*
1.	Hourly Speed Rate	$13\frac{1}{3}$ m	7 m
2.	Time Taken Per Mile	$\frac{3}{40}$ hr	$\frac{1}{7}$ hr
3.	Time Saved Per Mile	$\frac{31}{120}$ hr	$\frac{4}{21}$ hr
4.	Daily Passenger Miles Covered	52000 m	1480 m
5.	Time Saved Per day (3 x 4)	13433 hr	282 hr

(Time taken by a pedestrian to cover a mile $\frac{1}{3}$ rd hr.)

Valuation of Benefit Accruing to Passenger Traffic

The next step in the analysis is to attribute a value to a unit of time thus saved by an individual passenger. This brings us directly to the question of how this extra time is utilised. One can utilise it by working more and earning more. While another may like to save time just to avoid some strain of walking and enjoy leisure. The first one is an example of saving in working time while the other one is a case of saving in non-working time. These two categories should be treated differently while attributing value to a unit of time. Let us analyse the nature of time saving in this particular context. Consulting Table 8 we find that buses and cycles were widely used in that area. Compared to those two modes of transport, neither mileages covered nor number of passengers carried by other modes of conveyance, were significant. Moreover, since there was no arrangement of street lighting, traffic movement used to take place during day time. The traffic survey was carried on during a busy agriculture season. Buses were then crowded with agriculture labourers moving from place to place to attend to various work. There were commuters as also people representing land owning class, for whom time was precious in harvesting season. Cyclists too moved on errards. Relatively rich people could afford to make use of different types of vehicles and they did have the habit of taking pleasure trips or making journeys on special occasions. Hence journey made in vehicles other than bus or cycle are left out, since these were not work journeys as such. In this study only saving in working time is taken into consideration.

From the point of view of an individual the value of a unit of time of working time saved is the income expected to be derived from utilising the time in normal work. But in this particular case saving in time involves some cost, since the services of vehicles have to be paid for. As time saved is measured in hour unit, the value of working time saved to an individual should be the difference between his prospective hourly income and the actual cost incurred for saving an hour. From the fare structure of the bus route prevailing in 1970, fare per passenger mile was estimated to be nearly 4 paise. From Table 9 it appears that a habitual pedestrian, saved 31/120 hr per mile by travelling in bus. Therefore he was prepared to pay at least 4 paise to save 31/120 hr or alternatively 15 paise per an hour. Similarly, in case of cycle, hourly cost of saving time can be deduced from fare paid. Though cycles were normally owned by cyclists, a practice of hiring out cycles was prevalent in that area and the charge was 8 paise per hour in the locality, which can very well be taken as the hourly cost of using cycle as a mode of transport.

Now what is expected to be the hourly income of such a passenger? The annual per capita income figure published by the Bureau of Applied Economics and Statistics, Government of West Bengal was Rs. 562 in the year 1969-70. This may be accepted as the approximate level of per capita income of the people of West Bengal in January, 1970. Regular workers in the organised sector of the economy have 300 full working days, approximately (excluding 52 weekly holidays and a few statutory holidays). Taking normal working hours to be eight in this country, the most general per capita hourly income estimate comes to Rs. 562 ÷ (300 x 8) = 23 P. (twenty three paise in January, 1970). According to definition per capita income is total income divided by total population. Hence this estimate is modified a little to make it conform to the income of an employed person. From our village survey data we find that the average family size in the catchment area was 5. Hence, hourly family income comes to 5 x 23 P. = Rs. 1.15 in 1970. Taking account of all the members of a family we find, approximately 50 p.c. of them were engaged in different occupations. Therefore the hourly income estimate, for an employed person is 115 P. ÷ 2.5 = 46 P.

Total net gain accruing to the passengers of bus and cyclists on account of saving in time per day can next be obtained taking the difference between hourly income and hourly cost as the valuation unit. The results are presented in Table 2.10.

Assuming the same per capita hourly income for all able bodied persons the total value of time saved comes to Rs. 3203.54 per day.

Use of the same hourly income estimate for valuing total time saved, may be considered too simplistic. The village-survey data reveals that occupation structure in the adjoining village roughly had a pattern like this—owner cultivators 40 per cent, landless labourers 53 per cent and other occupations 7 per cent. By distributing the total time saved in proportion to the occupation structure, a different estimate of passenger traffic is prepared. In Burdwan district the statutory minimum wage for landless agricultural labourer was Rs. 3 per day in 1970. The working hours being 8 (eight), hourly income is equal to (300 P ÷ 8) = 37 P. But the point remains whether a labourer is expected to earn at this rate throughout the working period. In fact the unskilled labour market in agriculture sector is characterised by acute unemployment. The statutory wage rate does not reveal the true marginal productivity of labour. The labourers in their turn do not expect to get work at this rate every day. But they normally stick to job if it satisfies minimum consumption needs. In fact in the agriculture sector a fixed wage fund is distributed among total labourers engaged in production irrespective of their individual marginal productivity. The more the occupation is crowded, the lower will be the per capita income. The land owning class tries to allot as small an amount as possible to this wage fund and in no case it exceeds the total contribution of labourers to the production. Hence the hourly income figure is to be revised downwards.

Table 2.10 : Value of Time Saved Per Day (Single Income Estimate)

S. No.	*Item of Information*	*Types of Vehicle*	
		Bus	*Cycle*
1.	Hourly Cost	15 P	8 P
2.	Hourly Income	46 P	46 P
3.	Hourly Gain	31 P	38 P
4.	Hours Saved Per Day by Vehicle Users	13433 hr.	282 hr.
5.	Money Value of Time Saved (at 1970 Price Level)	Rs. 4164.23	Rs. 107.16
6.	Money Value of Time Saved (at 1965 Price Level)	Rs. 3123.17	80.37

Now as wage yields benefit to a wage earner, it is an important cost element in the production plan. There is a general practice in cost benefit analysis to introduce a shadow price of labour reflecting the real supply and dmand condition of the economy to correct imbalance in money cost. Such an equilibrium price is a better measure of prospective income. The movement of unskilled labourers from agriculture to construction work is common in a developing region. On the assumption that there is some loss of output in agriculture sector due to such transfers, the opportunity cost of unskilled labour is taken to be 50 p.c. of money cost in a report of Ministry of Transport[3] relating to a highway project in Burdwan district. In the absence of any other supporting data, half the hourly wage is accepted as the prospective income of a labourer in the ensuing analysis.

In case of owner cultivator the annual income estimate is obtained from the size of holding and net earning per acre. The size of holding per owner (3.5 acres of irrigated land and .48 acres of unirrigated land) is estimated from the village survey data. According to an estimate prepared by the Intensive Agricultural Development Project Office at Burdwan, annual net income from an acre of land producing paddy was 452.82 and that for wheat was Rs. 224.00 in 1969-70. Those figures hold for cultivators of average efficiency. Assuming double cropping in irrigated area and paddy cultivation only in unirrigated area, total annual income came to Rs. 2586.22 in 1969-70 (the assumption regarding cropping pattern is supported by both village survey and traffic survey data). As in the previous case total working hours for the entire year is taken to be 300 x 8 =2400 hr. Hence hourly income estimate comes to Rs. 1.07. For the remaining 7 p.c. of workers no income estimate is possible and therefore the old estimate of 46 P. is retained. The new benefit estimate is presented in Table 2.11. Applying the population weights to the hourly gain figures the last row is obtained. Hence hourly gain under bus and cycle come to 40.82 P and 47.82 P respectively. Using the saving in time figures provided in Table 2.9 total value for time saved under the two vehicle categories comes to Rs. 5485.35 and Rs. 134.85 at 1970 price level. Deflating them to 1965 price level we get the final estimates Rs. 4112.51 and Rs. 101.13 for two most common categories of passenger vehicles.

Table 2.11 : Value of Time Saved (Under Differential Income Estimate)

(in paise)

S. No.	Item of Information	Types of Vehicle					
		Bus			Cycle		
		Owner Cultivators	Labourers	Others	Owner Cultivators	Labourers	Others
1.	Hourly Cost	15	15	15	8	8	8
2.	Hourly Income	107	18.50	46	107	18.50	46
3.	Hourly Gain	92	3.50	31	99	10.50	38
4.	Weighted Hourly Gain	36.80	1.85	2.17	36.60	5.56	2.66

N.B.: Each item in row three (3) is multiplied by the percentage share of total population within that particular group in that area to obtain the figures in row four (4).

Combining the benefit estimates under all the different vehicle categories for commodity and passenger traffic, the overall benefit figures are obtained. Corresponding to different treatment of foreign exchange we get three estimates of commodity traffic benefit under motor vehicle category. Combining these three estimates with the two other estimates under passenger traffic altogether six estimates are presented in the next section. They are presented in Tables 2.12 and 2.13. The road length being 22.83 miles, the benefit and cost estimates are next reduced to per mile figures for calculating final ratios.

Table 2.12 : Total Daily and Annual Benefit (Under Single Income Estimate)

S. No.	Source of Benefit	Value of Benefit (in Rs.)		
		No Premium on F.E.	*50 P.C. Premium on F.E.*	*70 P.C. Premium on F.E.*
A.	*Commodity Traffic*			
1.	Motor Vehicle	107.16	117.37	122.25
2.	Animal Driven Vehicle	240.88	240.88	240.88
B.	*Passenger Traffic*			
3.	Bus	3123.17	3123.17	3123.17
4.	Cycle	80.37	80.37	80.37
5.	Total (Daily)	3551.58	3561.79	3566.67
6.	Total Annual	1296326.70	1300053.35	1301834.55
7.	Average Per Mile	56781.72	56944.95	57022.97

Table 2.13 : Total Daily and Annual Benefit (Under Differential Income Estimate)

S. No.	Source of Benefit	Value of Benefit (in Rs.)		
		No. Premium on F.E.	*50 P.C. Premium on F.E.*	*70 P.C. Premium on F.E.*
A.	*Commodity Traffic*			
1.	Motor Vehicle	107.16	117.37	122.25
2.	Animal Driven Vehicle	240.88	240.88	240.88
B.	*Passenger Traffic*			
3.	Bus	4112.51	4112.51	4112.51
4.	Cycle	101.13	101.13	101.13
5.	Total (Daily)	4561.68	4571.89	4576.77
6.	Total Annual	1665013.20	1668739.85	1670521.05
7.	Average Per Mile	72930.93	73094.16	73172.18

Traffic Forecasting and Measurement of Benefit Stream

The six estimates of prospective annual benefit, obtained under different assumptions, depend directly on the volume of traffic. We have intercepted traffic only once in 1970, a few years after the opening of the road. A set of data in respect of commodity movement is available for the year 1965. The big jump from 1965 to 1970 in commodity traffic shows that the economy of the catchment area was growing. Of course, these two sets of figures do not enable us to assume any particular form of trend for extrapolations since this big jump can only be attributed to the new facility created. At the same time we cannot reasonably hold that traffic flow will remain unchanged throughout the economic life period of the road. Transport investments do have a fairly long life period. In the earlier discussions, we have already noted that the benefit analysis in case of roads are normally carried over a period of 20 (twenty) to 40 (forty) years, though theoretically much longer technical life may be attributed to a road section. The annual benefit estimates have to be obtained for each particular year of the life period to get an idea of overall benefit. Hence arises the need for traffic forecasting.

Traffic forecasting involves an estimate of future level of production and consumption including exports and imports as also a similar estimate for population trend. From enquiries held at block level in respect of twenty sampled villages in the catchment area; it was found that population increased approximately at an annual rate of 3 p.c. to 3.5 p.c. during the period 1969 and 1974. The main productive activity in the area is agriculture, the principle crop grown being rice. Now area under cultivation during the same period grew by 19 per cent in the sampled villages as against an overall district figure of 11 per cent. A continuous series for rice production covering a period of 13 years (1960-61 to 1973-74) was collected from Intensive Area Development Programme Organisation of Burdwan District. An exponential trend is fitted to the series by least square method and the rate of growth is found to be 3.6 p.c. per annum. The official national income statistics of India, suggests that during

1968-73 growth rates in transport and agriculture sectors were almost on a par. These findings were kept in mind while attempting to forecast traffic along the road during next 40 years.

Since forecasting in the present case can only yield tentative results, we take two rates of growth (5 per cent and 3 per cent), the former on the high side and the latter on the low, to depict the prospective rate of growth of traffic along the M.K.M.M. road. Again as period under consideration is fairly long, it is quite possible that traffic growth will gradually peter out. Two types of treatment have been meted to each one of the six estimates. In one case it is assumed that the traffic will grow at the compound rate of 3 p.c. per annum for the first 10 years and then at 2 p.c. for the rest of the period under consideration. In another case the rates of growth are phased in the following manner - 5 p.c. per annum for the first 10 years, 4 p.c. for the next 10 years, 3 p.c. for the next 10 years, 2 p.c. for the last 10 years. The accumulated benefits have been intercepted at three stages after 20 years, 30 years and 40 years respectively.

Investment and Maintenance Cost

As per records of the office of Executive Engineer, P.W. (Roads) Burdwan, the M.K.M.M. road was declared complete and was opened to traffic in December 1965. The total cost of construction was reported to be Rs. 20,30,000. A discussion with the engineers in charge of construction revealed that technically it is possible to complete such an ordinary village road in 3 years and the cost can roughly be spread over in the following proportion. 35 per cent (1st year), 50 per cent (2nd year), 15 per cent (3rd year). To be precise, this is an estimated spread over of actual work and accordingly corresponds to distribution of inputs in real terms all of which are to be valued at 1965 price level. Though the accounting was completed in 1965, the actual work had been spread over for nearly nine years because of certain land acquisition problems. Annual expenditure or input consumption figures were not available. Hence we take Rs. 20,30,000 as the monetary investment cost in 1965 without any further adjustment and a 3 year cost phasing is introduced.

The benefit estimates are accordingly reduced to 1965 price level.

The data supplied by the P.W. (Roads) Department, West Bengal in 1970 suggests that in case of an ordinary road like this, labour cost constituted 10 p.c. of total cost. Of this total labour cost, according to engineers' opinion, 25 p.c. might be attributed to skilled labour. So far as skilled labour is concerned, we accept the prevailing wage rate as corresponding to the scarcity value of labour. But this rule cannot be applied to unskilled labourers in an area having surplus labour. If the unskilled labourers engaged in road construction were actually unemployed their alternative contribution would have been zero. We may at best assume that they were somehow engaged in agriculture, the principal sector in the region under discussion. In that case if they were transferred to the construction work, there might be some loss of output in the agricultural sector. Hence, it is not advisable to hold the opportunity cost of unskilled labour to be zero. However, it is not possible to estimate the real cost of transferring labour from agriculture to transport sector. Just as in the case of benefit estimate, the wage cost in unskilled labour category is thus deflated by 50 per cent following the practice accepted in the report on Durgapur-Express Way.

We may recall the special treatment meted out to foreign exchange component while preparing benefit estimates. Hence foreign exchange is to be treated separately in the cost side as well. The construction of ordinary roads generally do not require much foreign exchange. The main foreign exchange requirements relate to the import of construction machinery. The engineers held that foreign exchange component of such an ordinary road might roughly be taken as 7 p.c. of total material cost. The same adjustment as that of benefit side is introduced here as well. The results are presented in Table 2.14.

While investment cost is incurred once, a recurring maintenance cost is needed to preserve a road in usable condition. The categorywise breakup of maintenance cost was not available. It was reported that a fixed amount of Rs. 5000 per mile should be spent annually at the going price level during the economic life period of such a road. The fund had its sanction from the year on which the road was declared open to traffic. The foreign exchange involvement was negligible. The distribution between material and labour cost was same as construction cost according to the engineer's view. Making adjustment for cost on account of unskilled labour, the figure comes to Rs. 4812.50 per mile. This amount is assumed to remain unchanged throughout the life period of the project in the absence of any other information. Admittedly it is an instance of over simplification.

Table 2.14 : Category-wise Cost of Construction of M.K.M.M. Road

(in Rs.)

S. No.	*Item*	*Money Cost*	*Real Cost*		
			No Premium of Foreign Exchange	*50 P.C. Premium*	*70 P.C. Premium*
1.	Unskilled Labour	152250.00	76125.00	76125.00	76125.00
2.	Skilled Labour	50750.00	50750.00	50750.00	50750.00
3.	Total Labour Cost	203000.00	126875.00	126875.00	126875.00
4.	Indigenous Material	1699110.00	1699110.00	1699110.00	1699110.00
5.	Foreign Goods	127890.00	127890.00	191835.00	217413.00
6.	Total Material Cost	1827000.00	1827000.00	1890945.00	1916523.00
7.	Total Cost (3 + 6)	2030000.00	1953875.00	2017820.00	2043398.00
8.	Cost Per Mile		85583.66	88384.58	89504.94

Estimation of Benefit Cost Ratios

Using the formula derived in the previous chapter

$$\sum_{t=q+1}^{n+q} (B_t - O_t)(1+i)^{-t} \Big/ \sum_{t=1}^{q} K_t (1+i)^{-t}$$

where B_t, O_t, K_t stand for different values of annual benefit, annual maintenance cost and annual investment cost and i =rate of discount, q = gestation period and n=life period of the project, benefit cost ratios are next calculated and presented in Tables 2.15 and 2.16. The different values of benefit and cost are discounted back to the year t_o i.e., the year just preceding the starting of the project. Since 3 year investment cost phasing has been accepted benefit starts flowing from the fourth year and maintenance expenditure is supposed to be incurred continuously from the same year. Three different rates have been used for discounting purposes — 12 per cent, 10 per cent, and 8 per cent. In India, 12 per cent rate of discount is applied in most of the official reports in this period, on the plea that normal return to investment in this country is never lower than this. The argument developed earlier, sets two limits — 5 per cent to 6 per cent and 10 per cent for underdeveloped economies. Further, it is suggested that a premium may be added to account for uncertainty. Assuming 2 per cent premium for uncertainty, the upper and lower values are settled. The medium rate 10 per cent lies in between these two figures. Altogether 108 values of the ratio are deduced taking all these factors into consideration.

The main objective of the study is to lay bare the fact that the value of the ratio reacts to the assumptions that we make regarding different variables. These values are not to lead to any policy conclusion as this empirical study is not taken up with that purpose. The benefit estimates themselves mainly depend on two factors — per capita income and rate of traffic growth. The values of the ratio are presented under two headings benefit cost ratio under single income estimate and benefit cost ratio under differential income estimate. The values follow similar pattern, though the second set in buoyed to a higher level. The two rates of traffic growth evisaged are referred to as Case I and Case II, the former showing an annual rate of growth from 3 per cent to 2 per cent and the latter from 5 per cent to 2 per cent.

Table 2.15 : Benefit Cost Ratio (Under Single Income Estimate)

e^i	*Case I*			*Case II*		
	8	*10*	*12*	*8*	*10*	*12*
1	6.72	5.59	4.72	7.69	6.38	5.35
1.5	6.53	5.43	4.58	7.47	6.19	5.20
1.7	6.45	5.37	4.53	7.39	6.12	5.15
			n = 20			
1	8.41	6.63	5.37	9.39	7.42	6.01
1.5	8.19	6.45	5.21	9.12	7.21	5.84
1.7	8.08	6.37	5.15	9.02	7.13	5.77
			n = 30			
1	9.48	7.18	5.66	10.14	7.81	6.21
1.5	9.21	6.98	5.49	9.85	7.58	6.03
1.7	9.11	6.90	5.43	9.74	7.50	5.97
			n = 40			

Table 2.16 : Benefit Cost Ratio (Under Differential Income Estimate)

e^i	*Case I*			*Case II*		
	8	*10*	*12*	*8*	*10*	*12*
1	8.76	7.29	6.14	10.01	8.30	6.97
1.5	8.50	7.08	5. 97	9.72	8.05	6.76
1.7	8.40	7.00	5.90	9.60	7.96	6.69
			n = 20			
1	10.95	8.64	6.99	12.20	9.65	7.82
1.5	10.62	8.39	6.79	11.84	9.37	7.59
1.7	10.51	8.29	6.71	11.71	9.26	7.50
			n = 30			
1	12.33	9.35	7.36	13.18	10.15	8.08
1.5	11.97	9.08	7.15	12.79	9.86	7.84
1.7	11.83	8.97	7.07	12.65	9.74	7.75
			n = 40			

Finally, the sensitivity of the values of the ratio to changes in exogenous variables like rate of discount, shadow price of foreign exchange and life period may be discussed. Denoting the shadow price of foreign exchange by 'e' the two way tables are presented taking 3 x 3 values of i and e. These different sets are obtained at intervals of n = 20, n = 30 and n = 40. The values respond significantly to changes in rates of discount. They range from 4.72 to 9.48 in Case I and 5.35 to 10.14 in Case II under single income estimate for e =1. The corresponding ranges are 6.14 to 12.33 and 6.97 to 13.18 under differential income estimate. The lower limits occur at shorter time interval. The values rise monotonically with the length of life period and fall similarly with the increase in rate of discount. The responsiveness is less significant in the first case, the gap between highest and lowest values converging round 3 to 4. By and large, the sensitivity of the values of the ratio to e is not significant, though they show a declining tendency as higher premium is attached to foreign exchange. This is not surprising, since the import content of the project is almost negligible and so also its import saving potentiality. The highest and lowest values recorded under single income estimate are 10.14 and 4.53 respectively. The corresponding values under differential income estimate are 5.90 and 13.18. The lowest value occurs in Case I when i = 12, n = 20, e = 1.7. Similarly highest value is found in Case II when i = 8, n = 40, e = 1. Within these limits, a wide range of possibilities exist. The lists of values may be further lengthened by assigning some other values to the variables. But the task before an evaluator is to accept those assumptions which conform most to the economic realities of the situation and then consider the range of values. A decision based on a unique value of the ratio is open to question, since such exercises cannot be carried under controlled condition. As the values of the ratio are all through much above 1, the project is economically justifiable.

REFERENCES

1. Introduction to Transport Planning - United Nations (ECAFE).

2. *N.B.* : The manufacturing concerns of this country keep certain records for measuring the import content of their product from time to time. This is more or less a confidential affair. The figures quoted above were collected from reliable sources. But for obvious reasons the sources cannot be mentioned.
3. Economic Appraisal of Calcutta - Durgapur - Assansol Express way, 1968; Transport Research Wing (Ministry of Transport & Shipping) Govt. of India.

PART II

ASSESSING THE IMPACT OF A ROAD NETWORK

3

REGRESSION ANALYSIS

Functional Relationships of Economic Variables

While cost benefit analysis is a widely accepted method of project appraisal in transport sector, there is a second view that for development of rural roads, economic studies to estimate direct benefit and cost straightway will not be of much use. Some form of land access road (a kucha track connecting two habitation points) may be existing in almost every settlement. Transformation of this kucha track into an all weather access road with appropriate serviceability level exerts tremendous influence on the locality. It is expected to lower input cost, assure fair output price and expand market. Not only that, a social transformation may also take place by bringing the isolated villages in to contact with urban centre. Education, health and other facilities will open up. All these are often grouped as reorganisation benefit which will ultimately change the face of the economy. While such qualitative statements can be made rather easily, a rigorous analysis is needed to prove the hypothesis.

Economists make use of mathematical techniques for arriving at quantitative relations among different economic entities. Theoretical models are prepared to explain the functioning of a system. All models are however approximation to reality and are built on certain assumptions. They try to explain specific situations with reference to certain explanatory variables. In its simplest form models may contain certain identities or definitional relation, the most familiar of which is the national income identity expressed in the form $Y = C + I + G$. Where Y = gross national products, C = consumption expenditure; I =investment expenditure and G = government expenditure. Consumption and investment expenditures are in their turn explained with the help of behaviourial equations like $C = f\,[(1-k)y, r]$, where k is the rate of tax and hence $(1-k)y$ is disposable income and r is the rate of interest. Again $I = f\,(\Delta y, r)$ where Δy i.e. growth of GNP is a proxy for profit expectation and r is the rate of interest.

An Exposition of Simple Regression Analysis

Both linear and non-linear functions are fitted to economic variables for explaining a particular situation as well as indicating the effects of explanatory variables on a particular dependant variable. Not only the magnitude but the direction of variation are also important to explain a situation. Of the different techniques used by economists, regression analysis is widely used to explain the influence of one or more variables on a particular economic growth or welfare indicator. Illustrations of its use are found in time series consumption functions, demand functions and a host of such problems which lend themselves to statistical analysis. In its simplest form the quation is presented as $Y = A + Bx + e$. A common example in regression analysis is to find out the relation between height of fathers (X) and those of sons (Y). Corresponding to a particular value of father's height, there will be an associated value of height of son. The biological relationship does not exactly correspond to a mathematical function. If the figures are plotted in a diagram they form a band whose underlying tendency is to assume a linear form $\acute{Y} = a + bx$. But the values of $\acute{Y}$ will be a bit different from the values given in the series for Y. To intercept the underlying trend, it is advisable to choose a line or to choose values of a and b in such a way the deviation $Y- \acute{Y}$ becomes as small as possible. Ideally if $Y_i - \acute{Y}_i = e_i$ then $\sum_{i=1}^{n} e_i = O$ i.e. positive and negative deviation balance each other, with say 'n' observations.

Now $e_i = Y_i - \acute{Y}_i = Y_i - a — bx_i$, hence $\Sigma e_i =$

$$\Sigma e_i = \Sigma (Y_i — a — bx_i) = O \text{ or}$$
$$\Sigma Y_i = \Sigma a + b\Sigma x_i.$$

Dividing both sides by n we have, $\overline{Y} = a+b\overline{x}$. This gives us the equation of a line which passes through $\overline{x}, \overline{y}$ i.e. arithmetic means of given observations. Thus any line passing through ($\bar{x}$, $\bar{y}$,) will make the algebraic sum of the residuals zero, whatever be its slope. Hence, we do not get any specific line. For arriving at a unique solution least square criterion appears to be more powerful.

If each residual is squared, we get all non-negative quantities. The least square principle points out that a, b have to be selected in such a way as to minimise Σe_i^2 i.e. $\Sigma(Y_i - a - bx_i)^2$. Thus $\Sigma e^2 = f(a,b)$ since observations (Y_i, X_i) are given, so that passing of different lines through the scatter (i.e. taking different estimates for a and b) produces variation in the residual sum of squares. The necessary conditions for a stationary value are

$$\frac{\delta(\Sigma e^2)}{\delta a} = \frac{\delta(\Sigma e^2)}{\delta b} = o$$

i.e. Following the rules of partial derivation differentiating with respect to a and b

we have $\Sigma(y - a - bx) \times 1 = 0$

and $\Sigma x(y - a - bx) = 0$

or $\Sigma y = na + b\Sigma x$

$\Sigma xy = a\Sigma x + b\Sigma x^2$ These are called normal equations.

To arrive at a particular equation, we have to compute five quantities from the lists of observations. These are Σy, n, Σx, Σxy and Σx^2. Once these are obtained, the values of 'a' and 'b' can be easily computed. The least squares regression of y on x, becomes $\acute{y} = a + bx$ or $\acute{y} = Y + e = a + bx + e$, where e is a stochastic variable with a specified probability distribution. The purpose of the term is to point out the discrepancies that emerge between the observed values of y and the values of y that is to be given by an exact functional relationship.

Least square is one possible method of estimation. Other estimators may be there and other sets of equation like $\acute{Y} = a_1 + b_1x$ and $\acute{Y} = a_2 + b_2X$ may be obtained, following these methods. A generalised version of the model may be presented thus $y = \alpha + \beta x + \varepsilon$. Now samples are drawn from data generated by the above model in such a way that X values remain fixed from sample to sample. Then the only source of sampling variation is ε's which is reflected in the y's. Let us suppose that 100 samples of 10 pairs of X, Y values are drawn from the entire data. Thus 100 pairs of a, b can be estimated.

'a' and 'b' will have their sampling distributions. Now three measures of such sampling distribution are important to arrive at a unique estimator. These are the mean, the variance and the mean squared error. The mean value is the average yielded by the estimator in repeated applications. The bias is the difference between mean value and the parameter i.e. E(b)-(β) in case of co-efficient of X. If it is zero, the estimator is unbiased. The variance of the distribution measures the spread of the distribution about the mean value. Its square root i.e. standard deviation of the distribution is generally designated as standard error, in this case, of 'b'.

Most of the computer programmes for regression analysis along with the estimated values of b print out either its estimated standard error or else the ratio of b to its estimated standard error. This is normally called sample t statistics. If the sample t statistic is numerically higher than the preselected critical value of 't', as provided in tables supplying t values under different degrees of freedom (i.e. no. of equations—no. of variables) then it is concluded that X exerts influence on the value of Y, otherwise not. The significance of the relation can be tested at 1%, 5%, 10% level i.e. significance level of 1% means there is 99% chance of the relation being valid so forth and so on. This is the most elementary expositon of a simple regression analysis. But in economics, we are not fortunate enough to study the relationship between two variables under ideal conditions.

A More Elaborate Technique—Multiple Regression

Let us take the case of production of an agricultural commodity, say, paddy. It depends on quality of seed, timely supply of water, expertise of cultivators, soil condition and such other factors. If P denotes yield per acre of paddy and the different explanatory variables are designated by X_1, X_2, X_3 etc. then the functional relationship between input, output may take the following form $P = K + a_1X_1 + a_2X_2 + a_3X_3 + \ldots\ldots$ and we land into a realm of multiple regression.

The generalised version of a multiple regression equation may be put in the form $Y = \alpha + \beta_1X_1 + \beta_2X_2 + \beta_3X_3 + \ldots + \varepsilon$ where Y is the dependent variable and X_1, X_2, X_3 .... are explanatory variables. Since values of Y and X_1, X_2, X_3 ...... are available from the recorded data, the parameters β_1, β_2, β_3, ... etc. can be estimated with the help of differential equations. β_1, β_2, β_3 ... are called partial regression co-efficients. The interpretation of such a co-efficient is simple. For example β, measures the change in mean value of Y as a consequence of a change in X_1 by one unit, X_2, X_3 etc. remaining unchanged.

Safeguards to be Taken in Such an Analysis

Regression analysis is a powerful tool in the hands of economists for establishing cause effect relation among economic variables. To regress literally means to step back. Through a regression equation, therefore, the dependent variable is sought to be explained by moving backwards to explanatory variables. The development indicators can thus be explained as the result of movement in certain crucial factors.

But the usefulness of the analysis depends to a great extent on the choice of explanatory variables. One should avoid spurious relationships. For example, by chance a good fit may be derived between height of school students and size of class rooms in a particular school. But there is no point in developing such an analysis and the relationship may at best be assigned to chance factor.

Another point which has to be carefully tackled is the problem of multi-collinearity. The explanatory valiables may themselves be correlated. In that case the regression analysis will not be scientific. For example, production of a commodity is influenced by its input costs which again depend to some extent on transport cost. If at a particular point of time reduction in transport cost as a whole is taken as an explanatory variable, there is no point in taking lower input prices, item by item.

Just as in the case of cost benefit analysis a range of values of benefit cost ratio can be obtained under different assumptions and a unique solution is not encouraged, similarly in case of regression analysis also a rigorous relationship between dependent and explanatory variables is not contemplated. The 't' values indicate how far the relationship can be relied on. The relationship envisaged is an hypothesis and its reliability is put to test. The hypothesis is to be constructed after carefully studying the economic environment. The data which are to be utilised for estimating the parameters should also be generated carefully otherwise we shall not get a good fit. Since we assume road improvement along with some other factors bring in socio-economic reorganisation a regression analysis can be developed after selecting some indicators of reorganisation or development of the economy and listing a few explanatory variables along with road. While the set of valiables may vary from case to case, proximity to road will always be an explanatory variable in each case.

4

AN APPLICATION OF REGRESSION ANALYSIS TO A RURAL ROAD NETWORK

The Background

We have already presented a case study making use of cost benefit analysis. The study related to a road section in a rural area. We have intercepted direct vehicular benefit, though the possibility of exerting indirect influence on the economic environment has been hinted at. In this particular case, a compact area is taken up for purposes of our study. The point at issue is whether the existence of a pucca road exerts any influence on the economic development of an area. Certain indicators of economic development have been selected. Naturally, choice of such indicator depends on the economic characteristics of the region. Again, each one of the indicators is influenced not only by proximity to road, but also some other explanatory variables. Hence multiple regression analysis is suitable in such case.

There is almost a ten year gap between this and the earlier study. The venue has shifted. We are in Hoogly District adjacent to Burdwan. The area was found to be agriculturally prosperous and there was not much evidence of alternative occupation. In the former case, a road section running through different blocks was selected and the study related to the impact of its development on adjoining area. In the present study, a compact area was chosen. A road network was already existing and the question of developing the net work did not emerge. The analysis pinpointed the beneficial influence of road communication on important economic variable. Say, for example price of a major export crop. Village markets are not well organised. Farmers often do not get remunerative prices because of cunning operation of middlemen. The road side villagers usually get a price advantage because of lower transport cost and better link with market centre.

A cost benefit analysis can be taken up in respect of a road network. Also, regression analysis may be applied to a road section as well. The combination of the two techniques are best illustrated in the analysis followed in following papers. Messers Earter, Abel, Norton[1] developed a set of regression equations involving total value of crop output and a number of independent variables one of which is surfaced roads using data from western & eastern region of India. John Sprigg[2] made use of the regression coefficient developed in the earlier study to estimate the percentage increase in rice output resulting from 1% increase in surfaced road. The increase in rice output serves as a basic ingredient of benefit estimate for transforming kucha roads to surfaced roads in a wide area in the eastern India.

Some Basic Hypotheses

In this study an attempt is made to assess quantitatively the effect of proximity to pucca road on three selected growth indicators, namely, price of commercial crops, overall agriculture production and employment in non- agriculture sector. Incidentally, a few observations are also made on cropping pattern in relation to roads. The effect of road is sought to be analysed by fitting a few linear regression functions to village level data on farm-gate prices, per acre yield, relative acreages under different crops and share of a specific type of employment in total. Proximity to road is the common explanatory variable, while separate sets of independent variables have been included in each one of the equations. The idea behind this exposition is simply this. To start with it is useful to devise functional relationships between existence of pucca road and a few acceptable growth indicators rather than throwing our weight arbitrarily on road.

It is generally accepted that transport benefit arising out of improvement in road facilities is in course of time transmitted throughout the economy of the catchment area and ultimately exerts favourable influence on production. Production is diversified, production is increased. So the effect is felt on the traditional sectors and also new activities develop. Naturally, new employment opportunities open up. If the area is too much dependent on agriculture, there may be shift of people from primary, to say, tertiary sector. Further, improvement in road reduces unit cost of transport and ensures ease of mobility. As a result, agriculturists are likely to get a higher farm-gate price for their crops.

These effects are likely to be most potent when a virgin area is penetrated. In rural areas, feeder roads are expected to provide interconnection between villages and a central place, usually a market centre or an urban centre. Normally, the villages do possess an established agriculture sector as well as a set of existing alignments mostly discontinuous mud roads—with no other alternative transport facilities. When metal roads replace mud roads traffic composition changes completely. Animal driven vehicles are replaced by motor vehicles carrying bulk commodities and passengers. Headloading, similarly, yields place to bicycles. Thus improvement in farm to market road (i.e. market link road) is obviously beneficial to village economy.

Better communication system removes information gap and encourages villagers to adopt better technique of production. Supply of quality inputs is facilitated and may be procured at a reasonable price. There may be little scope for extension of cultivated area if land is already scarce, but a newly improved road is likely to encourage intensive cultivation. It may have effect on cropping pattern—the exact nature of which is to be probed. Apart from such economic benefits, roads also provide opportunities for social amenities. But for the present, we are concentrating on economic variables only.

However, at the outset, one particular point needs to be clarified. Production, price, employment and such other variables depend on a number of factors other than road. For example, agriculture depends on supply of inputs like fertiliser, irrigation, quality seeds; environmental factors like soil and climate as also on other infrastructural facility like credit institution, storage, etc. Moreover, investment in road is almost always accompanied by a package of complementary investments for utilisation of production potentialities of the area. So the resulting growth comes from all the factors taken together and isolating the effect of one item is difficult. The multi-variate regression analysis helps us in this respect in as much as we can have an insight on road effect exclusively while taking into account the role of other relevant factors as well.

The approach differs from traditional economic analysis of highway projects in two respects. First, it focuses on development benefit to the exclusion of road user benefit. In fact, the traditional analysis based on quantification of road user benefit can hardly be logically extended to rural feeder roads. The average volume of daily traffic on such roads is often quite low, and the new traffic pattern that they generate has such far reaching socio-economic effects that they cannot be fully captured in road user benefit. Secondly, highway project analysis is normally carried on with reference to road sections rather than to road network. Since arterial connects nodal points and caters to fast moving long distance traffic sectional approach concentrating on road user benefit may have its justification. But for feeder roads, the influence of one road section cannot be studied effectively in isolation. It is more relevant to study the effect of road infrastructure in a compact, homogeneous area i.e. the entire analysis is to be fitted in a regional framework however small the area of influence may be. That is why we have selected one Block area to study some of the likely effects on a number of feeder roads on the villages lying within its administrative boundary. There are two reasons for making this choice. First, a block is the base area unit for planning in rural areas in our country. Secondly, being the lowest administrative unit, the villages within the block form a more or less homogeneous compact area, with villagers sharing some common interests regarding general infrastructural facilities.

The Project Area

The Block-Pursuah-in Hooghly District, West Bengal was selected for this study. It has an area of 100.5 Sq.Km. comprising fifty (50) villages within it. The density of population was 968 per Sq.Km. according to 1971 census, fairly high compared to density of rural population (698) in Hooghly District. The main road a state highway, passes just through the middle of it connecting two urban centres on either side of the block. The block office as well as the main commercial centre is situated on this road, though the later is not within the administrative jurisdiction of the block. This is the present situation also, though some other improvement has taken place in the last twelve years. Roads taken up at that time have been completed. In 1978-79 it was found that two link roads (both surfaced) were already there in the southern part of the block, while one was under construction in the northern part. The total length of surfaced road running through the block was found to be 21 miles or 33.6 Km. The fifty villages comprising the block were all located within a distance of not more than 12 Kms. from a pucca road. Excepting a few ferry services which mostly operated during rainy season, the block had no other means of communication.

The economy was entirely agro-based, the principal crops being paddy and potato. While paddy was used almost entirely for internal consumption, 90 per cent of potato crop was being marketed by the cultivators. As for other crops, jute came next in importance to potato. The area under aman paddy had been 36.65% of the gross area under cultivation followed by potato (28.19%), jute (10.00%) and oil seed (6.77%). The rest of the area was taken up by boro paddy, vegetables, wheat and pulses. Seventyone per cent of the total area is reported to be under cultivation in the block report of 1977-78 and the cropping intensity was little above 200 at that time.

The area being flood prone, the yield of aman paddy was uncertain. People relied more on commercial crops, specially potato. The area had potentiality of producing two other perishable but remunerative products—fish and vegetable as the general conditions suggested. The new roads sought to improve villagers' link with nearby market centre. Some storage facilities were also built up on road side villages, though their capacities were inadequate according to the villagers. Another important development subsequent to road improvement was the emergence of road-side sub-centres, where middlemen collected their stocks. All these developments appeared to have contributed to the prospect of marketability of agriculture surplus of the area.

The villages in the Block had little infrastructural facilities excepting that 67 per cent of the net area under cultivation was irrigated. Interestingly enough, most of other facilities were coinciding with the existence of pucca road. Six cold storages and twelve small shopping-cum-service centres came up alongside road. Out of nineteen post offices, as many as eleven were situated in villages having pucca road. The generation of fast moving traffic like buses, trucks, cycles along pucca road greatly increased the mobility of men and goods. Bicycles were found to be extremely popular with villagers. The maximum distance of a village from the nearest urban centre was found to be 20 Km., the major concentration being within the range of 10 to 20 Km. This distance is easily negotiable by fast moving vehicles provided the road condition is satisfactory. Now, the point at issue is whether villages having improved links with nodes like market centre and urban centre are really better off than their counterparts having kucha links only. To have a clear idea of the issue, data on specific aspects were collected from all the villages.

Village-wise data on cultivated area, irrigated area and crop yield were available at the Block office. Farm gate prices for two major commercial crops-potato and jute — at a particular point of time, no. of households, occupational classification of working population and sundry other information about village economy were collected through Gram Sabha representatives. The District Agriculture Marketing Office, Hooghly supplied the price data for valuing crop yield [Output of each crop is valued at annual average price for the product prevailing at the market centre commonly used by the villages]. The values of the most crucial explanatory variable, distance of each village from pucca road, were recorded from the block level road map provided by P.W. (Roads) Office, Hooghly District. The yield and area figures relate to 1977-78, since the entire area was flooded in 1978 and 1978-79 cannot be regarded as a normal year. The road network depicts the position in March 1979, while the rest of the village data relate either to March or to June 1979. The data are by no means adequate and proxy variables are used to fill in the gap. But that is a common problem in almost all Socio-economic analysis.

A clear notion of the relavant relations is an important ingredient of econometric analysis. A statistical fit may not always give an undisputed pattern of causation. However, the strength of the argument lies in the fact that the pattern is also expected to come out on direct economic and social reasoning. With this background in mind we proceed with our hypotheses relating to the set of rural growth indicators so to say.

Testing the Hypotheses

Farm-Gate Prices

As has been already stated, the traditional major commercial crops in the area were potato and jute. The farm gate price of each one of these two crops in the post harvest period was collected from each of the fifty village. The data presented variation in prices of these products from village to village, being generally higher in road side villages. But in each case, it was lower than that which prevailed at the nearest market centre. The market centre was found to be large and fed by several villages in the neighbourhood apart from those lying in the selected block. It is presumed that the centre was in a position to absorb the entire output of the block at quoted prices. In fact, the agents of the dealers in the market centre used to procure bulk of the commodities from the villages, quoting different prices at different villages.

Since the market demand force is expected already to be taken care of in the quoted price, the price is to be related to supply factors like the level of production, cost of production, cost of transport, institutional facility. Soil condition, rainfall as also irrigation being almost uniform in the area, cost of production is expected to vary according to price and availability of inputs like seeds, fertiliser, pesticides, etc. Thus the cost of production which depends on price of inputs and cost of transport for marketing output are both dependent on the road factor. Road side collection centre run by the dealer's agent is surely an institutional improvement. So finally the following factors are selected to explain the prices of two commodities, potato and jute. The two functions are :–

i) pv =F(v, r, D); and ii) pj = F(J, r, D)

where

Pv = farm gate price of potato per qtl. in each village
pj = farm gate price of jute per qtl. in each village
v = per capita output in qtl. of potato in each village
J = total output in qtl. of jute in each village
r = distance in Km. of each village from pucca road
D = dummy for road side collection centre, taking the value '1' for village using the facility, 'O' for others not having the facility.

Potato is a vegetable and part of it was consumed locally as also a certain percentage of output was kept as seeds. So it is scaled to population. Jute was almost entirely sold out, cultivators preferred to buy quality seeds from market. Hence total output is taken here. The factors influencing supply viz., variation in input cost and cost of taking the output to the market are subsumed under distance variable. It is expected that the further is the village from pucca road, the lower will be the farm gate prices prevailing there. The villages using subcentre facilities will enjoy a higher price. Finally, bigger supply is likely to lower price.

From data relating to fifty villages, the following price equations are estimated :-

i) $p_v = 35.00 + .10v - 1.67r + 3.44D$ $\quad R^2 = 0.38$
(.6642) (-3.825) (3.390) $\quad F = 9.416$
$DF = 3,46$

ii) $p_j = 168.98 + 837.53J - 2.47r + 7.24D$ $\quad R^2 = .22$
(.4426) (-2.202) (-2.733) $\quad F = 4.444$
$DF = 3,46$

[Figures in brackets are the respective t values]. The co-efficients of r and D are found to be significant at 1 per cent level in both the cases. Thus while our hypotheses regarding 'r' and 'D' are being supported by the data, the level of production is not showing the expected relationship. Even the sign is going contrary to accepted norm of price fixation equation. Possibly, as each village supplies a small quantity of the total, they are not able to affect the price.

Agriculture Production

After prices we turn to agriculture production. Agriculture is the principal occupation and therefore the first indication of growth is likely to come via an increase in agricultural output. As has been already noted, apart from traditional factors land and labour, agriculture depends on supply of inputs like fertiliser, quality seeds, the level of technology, environmental factors like soil types, rainfall etc.; and infrastructural facility like irrigation transportation and markets.

Since the equation is fitted to the village-wise data of a particular block in a particular year, we assume that environmental factor and technology are almost uniform. The percentage of irrigated area is fairly high and it does not seem to have been affected by road, the correlation coefficient between the two being .06. So apart from land and labour we have taken only irrigation. The supplies of recurring inputs are themselves influenced by the distance variable to a considerable extent and so they are not separately introduced in the equation.

The yield function is formulated thus $Y = F(L, I, r)$

where

Y = value of per acre yield of all crops in each village
L = No. of persons engaged per acre of gross cultivated area in each village
I = area irrigated per acre of gross cropped area in each village
r = distance of each village from pucca road

L is a proxy variable for agriculture labour. Data regarding inflow of casual labour to the area are not available and since owner cultivators themselves are engaged in agricultural operation and always do some supervision we have taken the entire working population in the agriculture sector. The figures in this category relate to June 1979, where as yield and area figures are for the previous year.

The estimated equation is as follows :-

$$Y = 1202 + 85.01L + 3286.87I - 47.00r \qquad R^2 = .25$$
$$(.9096)\ (3.338)\ (-1.307) \qquad F = 5.220$$
$$DF = 3.46$$

It appears that overall yield in agriculture sector is negatively related to the distance factor and the relationship is significant at 10 per cent level. We may conclude that villages nearer to pucca road enjoy a comparatively higher yield i.e. agriculture productivity is influenced by good accessibility. Irrigation is positively and quite significantly (at 1% level) related to agriculture production, which is what anybody should expect. The coefficient of labour is not significant but carries the right sign. This may be due to the weakness in our selection of the variable.

Cropping Pattern

The yield function suggests that agriculture productivity is higher in villages nearer to pucca road. One may also expect that existence of pucca road influences cropping pattern. For example, the common feeling may be that villages nearer to pucca road go for the cultivation of commercial crops in a much more wide scale. But we do not think that proximity to pucca road is a decisive factor with regard to choice of cropping pattern, which is primarily dependent on soil and climatic condition. When there is little scope for breaking new soils, relative prices of different crops rather than their absolute prices affect farmers' decision. If jute is expected to fetch higher price than aus paddy is a particular year, acreages under jute will increase at the expense of those under aus paddy. In a particular Block, distance from road affects absolute price of all commodities via its influence on transport cost. But so far as relative prices are concerned, they do not seem to be affected so much i.e. Nearer the village is to a pucca road, the higher is the farm gate price for every crop be it potato, paddy or anything else. But the ratio between prices of any two crops is not likely to vary significantly from village to village.

However, we have tried to analyse the effect of pucca road on cropping pattern by selecting three important crops in the region viz, potato, jute and paddy. According to hypothesis, villages nearer to road will bring more acreages under potato and jute while villages further off will take to subsistence farming i.e. paddy cultivation. Apart from road we have taken only another factor irrigation, which is also deemed to be an infrastructural facility.

Sticking to our earlier assumption of homogeneity of soil, uniformity of climate etc., the following functions are envisaged.

i) $A_v = F(r, I)$ ii) $A_j = F(r, I)$ and iii) $A_p = (r, I)$

where

- Av - area under potato as a proportion to gross area under cultivation
- Aj - area under jute as a proportion to gross area under cultivation
- Ap - area under paddy as a proportion to gross area under cultivation
- I - area under irrigation as a proportion to gross area under cultivation
- r - distance of each village from pucca road.

The estimated equation for potato gives a good fit.

$$A_v = -3.61 - 275.04r + .57I \qquad R^2 = .52$$
$$(-9.540)\ (7.220) \qquad F = 26,19$$
$$DF = 2,47$$

The coefficients of both r and I are highly significant implying that road side villages have proportionately greater areas under potato which needs bulk movement. That potato needs irrigation is a well recognised fact which is also substantiated here. But the fit in respect of jute is far from satisfactory. The estimated equation is

$$A_j = 0.27 + 2217.16r - 0.31I$$
$$(1.104)\ (-5.760)$$

The coefficients or r and I are not significant, even the signs are contrary to general hypothesis. Further, we can hardly generalise the road effect if we examine the third equation which runs thus —

$$A_P = .58 - 19.41r - .12I \qquad R^2 = .09$$
$$(-.8614) \qquad (-2.10) \qquad F = 2.485$$
$$DF = 2{,}47$$

clearly the two explanatory variables are not sufficient to explain the relative acreage under paddy. According to hypothesis, the co-efficient of 'r' should have a positive sign, implying greater acreage under paddy in distant villages. But this is not the case. The negative and significant coefficient of 'I' suggests that paddy cultivation does have inverse relation with irrigation. The area being flood prone and the acreage under 'boro paddy' being very small, this seems to be quite plausible.

Occupation Structure

Now coming to the occupation structure of this thickly populated area we find that the share of agriculture force in total working population was as high as 74% at the time of enquiry. But it is likely that improvement in roads, apart from boosting up agriculture may offer new employment opportunity to the people of the area at least in the tertiary sector. For example, as new modes of transport like buses, trucks and cycles were introduced, road side cycle repairshops, motor mechanic shop made their appearance. Tea and snack shops opened up doing good business catering to the needs of passengers and transport operators. The roadside sub-centres for collecting commercial crops also used to offer some employment opportunity. Hence, it may be expected that villages lying nearer to pucca road would have more people engaged in non-agriculture sector.

Of course, the manpower demand in agriculture sector, which mainly depends on area under cultivation first draws the working population Moreover, when agriculture is remunerative, i.e. area grows commercial crop to a larger extent, the share of non-agricultural population in total working force is likely to be smaller. In our analysis the occupation function stands thus—

$$NW = F(AW, SC, r)$$

where

NW - share of non-agricultural worker in total working population

AW - per capita availability of land for working population in each village

SC - share of commercial crop in total value of crops in each village

r - distance of each village from pucca road

The estimated equation gives the following result —

$$NW = .37 - 8.12AW - .16SC - 3.00r \qquad R^2 = .20$$
$$(-.5290)\ (-.8153)\ (-3.244) \qquad F = 3.908$$
$$DF = 3{,}46$$

The coefficient of distance variable is significant at 1% level. The coefficients of two other variables are not significant, but they have the right signs. So road seems to be exerting its influence on occupation structure, opening up opportunities for diversification in employment. This is no doubt an encouraging trend in an area with a heavy pressure of population on land.

Summing Up

We may now sum up by saying a few words on the twofold objective of the exercise. The set of equations presented in the last section provides answers to two basic questions. First, whether building of pucca roads really influence crucial growth factors in a rural economy. Secondly, how the specific contribution of roads to economic development can be assessed quantitatively, so that we may not have to throw our weight arbitrarily on road.

Certain pattern has emerged in the estimated equations namely, villages nearer to pucca road are in a relatively advantageous position with respect to farm gate prices of their product. Moreover, pucca roads favourably affect agricultural activity and offer new employment opportunities.

Finally, the coefficient of 'r' in each one of the equations tells us by what amount the dependent variable will change in response to a unit change in 'r' when other explanatory variables are maintained at given levels. Thus changes in production, employment etc. due to the construction of pucca roads can be measured in exact quantitative terms. The coefficients have been used in the following exercise to forecast future level of agriculture production and employment in non-agriculture sector.

However, the experiment has been made in a very limited scale. Any generalisation regarding road effect should possibly have to be based on more experiments of this type. Different blocks having different levels of penetration as well as different levels of activity may be subjected to this type of analysis so that a definite conclusion can be reached regarding its utility. With widening of choice of area and deeper probing, we expect better results. Some other growth indicators may also be picked up and surely explanatory variables need further refinement. To achieve this standard, we should think in terms of generating data more comprehensively. Analytical models for assessment of road projects are scarcely suited for universal application. But the regression model is surely an effective method of assessing road effect.

REFERENCES

1. Easter, Abel & Norton — Regional differences in agricultural productivity in selected areas of India-American Journal of Agricultural Economics, May 77, Vol. 59, No. 2.
2. John Sprigg–Benefit cost analysis of surfaced roads in the eastern rice region of India — American Journal of Agricultural Economics, same issue.

PART III

A SCREENING CRITERION FOR A NETWORK PLAN

5

WEIGHTED RATING METHOD

General Observations on Rural Road Planning

The two types-of-analysis-developed so far are quite comprehensive but a bit complicated. The cost benefit analysis has been applied to a road section. If instead of a road section, we have to pass judgement on a road network involving different road sections, the analysis can be applied separately for each section and a ranking of values thus obtained will help *inter se* priority determination of individual projects to be implemented. Alternatively, perspective benefit to be derived from the entire system may be estimated and compared to the cost involved in improving the network. This is useful when the issue is to form a judgement on provision of infrastructure in the context of area planning.

One of the most important condition for the growth of rural areas is to ensure mobility for men, technology and finished goods. The only infrastructure that provides this facility is all weather good roads. Hence arises the demand for a suitable network. Now a well thought out plan may involve some or all of the following steps. The first step involves collection of data for making an idea of quantum of investment on and socio-economic impact of a road network in a compact rural area. Next, regression models may be developed to identify important variables that accelerate rural growth. The role of road network in the development process can be separately assessed in the process. Following this logic, a simulation model may be designed to correlate the scale of rural development with the structure of road network. This model may be used to identify the variables to study the optimum investment in the selected area for the existing road network or to develop the appropriate network for planned investment in different socio-economic activities within the same area. From the above model suitable criterion for future road network may be evolved.

The inventory of data thus collected normally consists of secondary information on the existing socio-economic background of the people including income and employment situation, past achievements in productivity, future prospect for production in different sectors, provision of better inputs, modern technology etc. Simultaneously, an inventory of the existing road network within an administrative unit say, a block is to be formed to evaluate the present accessibility between villages, both large and small and between villages and markets, small towns and the arterials like major district roads or state highways. The existing conditions of road whether they are metalled, gravel or dirt roads should be noted. While suggesting development at local level an idea of prospective benefit may be formed. The direct benefit is derived from cost saving on normal traffic and generation of new traffic. The indirect benefit includes net value added to total production. In the second case the share of road improvement in additional production can be estimated with the help of suitable regression co-efficient. The suggested improvements for which cost estimates are always made can then be justified by applying cost benefit criterion to each individual project. But this is surely an elaborate process.

The Practice in India

However some exercises are always taken recourse to while chalking out a road plan. At this stage, we may refer to broad policies that have since been followed in this sphere in our country. The present road system in India has been built up, following the norms laid down in two perspective plan namely, Nagpur Plan 1943 and Twenty Years' (1961-1981) Plan laid down in Chief Engineers' Report 1958. The formulae presented in these plans were developed on the basis of fixed weightages attached to population size. In fact, habitations have been classified according to the size of population. The larger the size, the greater is the weightage. Some allowance has been given to expected future rate of growth of agriculture and industry. It may not be out of place to mention here the broad policy recommendation of Chief Engineers' Report[1] in respect of road system in a rural area. The objective outlined is to bring every village : (a) in a developed and agricultural area within 4 miles of a metalled road and 1.5 miles of any road; (b) in a semi-developed area within 8 miles of a metalled road and 3 miles of any road; and (c) in an underdeveloped and uncultivable area within 12 miles of metalled road and 5 miles of any road. Thus the emphasis is clearly on agricultural areas. However, rural roads are only a part of their overall interest namely, building a viable road infrastructure for the entire country.

In 1967, a one man committee on Rural Road[2] was appointed specially for going into the details of rural road system in this country. One of its terms of reference has been to indicate the basis for determining *inter se* priority between various categories of rural roads in the state. The committee accepted the mileage target of village roads laid down in the Chief Engineers' Report. As for priority determination, it rated highest "areas where special steps have already been taken for rapid increase in agriculture production". Of course backward areas and areas with no other means of transport (the two are likely to be overlapping) were mentioned separately in the rating list and each received half of the weightage attached to the agri-culturally prosperous areas. Thus in all these reports, we find mainly two factors -- population and agriculture -- being considered for road planning in rural area. The minimum needs programme under Fifth Five Year Plan laid down the principle of linking up villages with a population of 1500 or above with improved road system by 1978. The Sixth Plan further stressed that villages having a population between 1000 and 1500 should also be connected with improved road system.

In principle it is to be accepted that all human settlement require to be provided with at least some form of all weather access road as a basic infrastructural facility. But population alone cannot guide all decisions. Depending on resource position and the overall activity level of different areas, a step by step approach is, however, called for. Since there may be competing claims, for all practical purposes it is better to have a simple criterion for priority determination. Rural roads cannot always be justified by the volume of traffic they are expected to bear. Hence a screening criterion based on road user benefit, which is quite popular with highway project analysis can hardly be copied here without reservation. The interdependence of transport and production, of transport and social services in the rural environment is to be understood in proper perspective before a decision can be made. The stress should be on overall developmental impact of a road section or a road network on its catchment area. Now all factors are not equally important in the development process of an area. So, the choice of factors are to be made carefully. In fact while broad principles have been laid down in perspective plans, models are being put to test within smaller area units. The emphasis on population and agriculture is justified at macro-level since agriculture is the main occupation in rural areas of India. But at a micro-level a more cautious approach should be developed and a wide range of factor should be taken into consideration. For easier and wider applicability the technique should be simple and should not require any elaborate data collection. But that does not mean leaving out essential information.

Ellet Model of Walters

Any road network starts with a design of connecting important nodes through arterials and then linking suitable points in the catchment area with arterials through feeder raods. Unless the feeder roads are properly planned, arterials remain underutilised. Also the potentialities of the catchment area remain unexplored. That the ease and cost of mobility have something to do with market extension and hence adds to production incentive is a recognised fact. The basic Ellet Model presented by Walters[3] gives the idea in a nutshell.

The model relates to an area having the same rainfall and soil conditions and depending on subsistance agriculture. It takes up the cultivation of a commercial crop say rubber to be sold to a port P at a fixed price of K per ton. The initial assumptions are the shadow price of additional labour from the existing work force is zero and none can walk diagonally in a NE - SW or SW - NE direction. From the port P, a road is

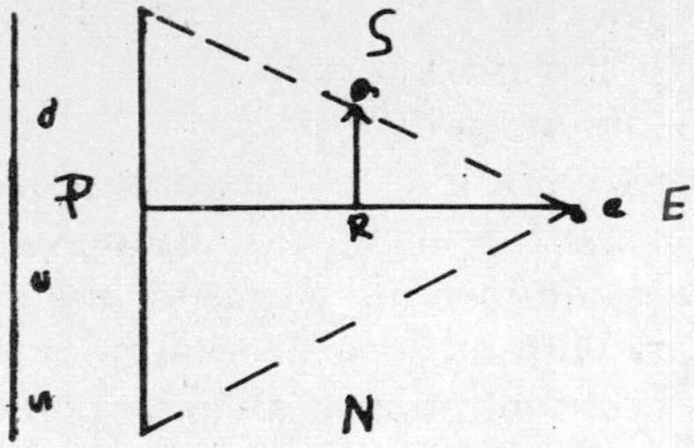

Figure 5.1
Q is a point from which rubber is transported to P with the help of both method such that QR = d_1 (head loading) and PR = d'_1 (motor transport)

constructed towards east, perpendicularly to the coastline. Now, farms laying on east, north south of P (sea is on the west) can send their supplies to P and they will do so provided the price prevailing at P is less than or equal to the cost of transporting the goods at P. Now, porters can carry goods on their heads to P from certain points and after the construction of the road goods may also be carried in motor vehicle from places on the road. The advantage of building the road is that supplies can be brought to different points on the road, instead of carried to the port direct through head loading. The costs of head loading and motor transport are fixed at Ṣb and Ṣa per ton mile respectively.

Now if there is only one mode of transport then the limit of farming is reached at the point d, where K = bd in case of head loading and at the point d', where K = ad' in case of motor transport. The exposition implies that Ṣb >Ṣa, and hence $\frac{K}{b}$ or d < $\frac{K}{a}$ or d'. Thus with the construction of road, the farming area will increase. Moreover, the two transport modes will be used simultaneously and farming will extend up to $d_i + d_j'$, on all sides such that $K \leq \frac{bdi+adj}{dj}$ always, for each farm's product. Walters has given several variants of this basic model. As regards feeder roads connecting agricultural areas to an arterial, he has come to the conclusion, that they open up new fields and also enable farms to enjoy cost reductions on existing traffic. But the overall benefit is less than that offered in pure development case. The emphasis is clearly on the role of road transport on marketability of product -- transport cost being treated as conditioning supply to a large extent.

However, roads cater to two way traffic. Just as surplus products are sent to the market, goods also move into the region. People move about on different errands as well. Infact, the design of road net work is to be based logically on an estimate of overall transport demand. For example, let us think in terms of a compact administrative unit for the purpose. Initially one has to start with an idea of total population of the area and its degree of concentration at different points. The locations of production centres; both existing and potential, have to be ascertained. Further, it is better to have also reliable estimates of output generated in these sectors and the level of internal consumption so that finally one can have a fairly good forecasting of exports from and imports to the region. Similarly the travel needs of the people can be estimated, at least roughly, from occupational pattern, social habits, location of social service centres etc. Finally, population and output data have to be translated into traffic, both by volume and by origin destination so that a network most convenient for the locality may be devised. But such a step by step procedure can hardly be followed in rural road planning, if not for anything else but practical difficulties. The task of generating and tackling so much of data is stupendous.

In case of rural roads, the planner often starts from a set of existing alignments — mostly discontinuous mud roads with no other alternative transport facilities. He may have to face a number of competing claims for improving these alignments. He cannot go by estimating prospective road user benefit. Normally the average daily traffic volume is low in rural areas. Moreover, where metal roads replace mud roads traffic composition changes completely. Animal driven vehicles are replaced by motor vehicles carrying bulk commodities and passengers. Headloading similarly, yields place to bicycles. The change in traffic composition increases the ease and speed of journey and may effect overall level of economic activities in the adjoining area. Normally, the villages do possess an established agriculture sector and developmental investment may have already taken place simultaneously with improvement in road. So farm to market type of road will exert a favourable influence. There may be little scope for extension of farm area, but a newly improved road is likely to encourage intensive cultivation as well as diversification of production. Apart from obvious economic benefits, roads also open up opportunities for social amenities. All such possibilities of favourable impacts are to be taken into account in formulating road plans.

The interdependence of transport and agricultural production systems in the rural environment is a recognised fact. Since quantification of road users' savings has little significance for such roads a way out will be to analyse the mechanisms by which transport cost savings are translated into increased production as also full utilisation of resources. This amounts to catching net development benefit, by estimating net increase in production running through the life period — of project and comparing it with investment and maintenance cost incurred for the same period. But it may not be worthwhile to take up such laborious procedure for all projects, big or small. Moreover, this procedure has the risk of overstressing benefit without making due allowances to complementary investments that may take place simultaneously. Though priorities may be assigned on the strength of estimated values of NPV or benefit cost ratio, a simple rough and ready method may be more suitable for all practical purposes, specially while dealing with small feeder road projects in rural areas.

Weighted Rating Method and Network Plan

The weightened rating method[4] is such a simple and flexible technique. As has been already pointed out a net work plan for rural road cannot be taken up in isolation. It is a part of integrated development of rural areas. The population, an exogenous variable, produces a demand for transport. The settlements within one particular administrative unit may be of varying size and importance. Basically the problem is to choose a few important nodes and connect all settlements with them. In rural areas, the greatest need is to facilitate mobilisation and marketing of agricultural surpluses and ensuring fair prices to primary producers. So the most important mode is the market centre which normally has a semi-urban character now-a-days. Incidentally it may have some other facilities like a health centre, a higher secondary school or a cinema house etc. The more it takes up an urban character, the greater will be the available facilities. From the point of view of rural economy this is a growth centre. Like market centre, administrative centre is also accepted as a node. Sometimes the two nodes may coincide. When the two are different, they may share the pride of having other infrastructural facilities mentioned above. Geographically, it is neither feasible nor desirable that all roads leading to different directions start from one and the same nodal centre, though as many settlements as possible, should have good access to it. One may logically start with a road joining two nodes say one marketing-cum-urban centre and one administrative centre. This should be of higher specification, an arterial expecting to bear more or less heavy traffic. The feeder roads will intersect it at several points, so that the nodes become ultimately accessible to most of the settlements via pucca road.

A rational screening criterion should be there to select suitable framework for a particular area. The criterion is to take into account not only economic but also extra economic factors because road's influence extends beyond pure economic considerations. The weighted rating method which is suggested here is based on the importance attached to different economic and non-economic factors by the planners and therefore it is partly psychological. Naturally, the weights are to be deduced after carefully considering national and regional objectives in view of the society. There may be some common factors worth considering in each case. But there may be others which have relevance for specific cases only. So choice of factors and of weights may vary from case to case, though the basic reasoning remains the same.

Since road development cannot be thought of independently and in isolation of general economic condition, the choice of a framework presupposes full knowledge of socio-economic condition of the area. It may be preceded by a regional survey yielding information on resource position, productive structure, infrastructural facility, location of educational, medical or communication centres etc. It will be further helpful if an opinion survey of the people can be made, regarding choice of alignment. The main factors to be taken into consideration are population, production pattern, production potentialities, cost of providing the road facility as also improvement in connectivity. Each one of these factors does have sub-categories and the choice of sub-categories will differ from case to case depending on characteristics of the region through which the road passes.

The following steps are commonly involved in this method. The factors that are taken into consideration should be expressed in terms of specific measuring units. Items like population, output etc., offer not much of a difficulty. For qualitative factors mostly coming under the category connectivity, specific alternatives will have to be suggested, so that at least arbitrary values may be attached to them. The second step in the analysis is to provide a common rating scale. The measuring units of the factor are different and often range of values are quite large. For example agricultural output amounts to thousands of tons, population figures may also be quite large. To bring heterogeneous, large factor values to commensurate term, a common rating scale lying between 0 and 100 is to be employed. It can bring within it both quantitative and qualitative factors. For example,

1. Population per Km of road (quantitative)

Range of factor values	0	5000	10,000
Common rating scale	0	50	100

2. Existence of parallel road at a distance (qualitative)

Range of factor values	within 2 km	within 5 km	above 5 km
Common rating scale	0	50	100

so fourth and so on.

Once the factors are thus reduced to manageable forms, the next step is to assign relative weight to each factor. The weightage is given on a percentage basis. But assigning weights to particular factor is the most complicated part of the entire exercise. The priority to be assigned to different projects will depend to a large extent to the weighting system chosen thus. While factor values have factual basis, the weighting system is psychological and it depends on planner's value judgements. To be on the safe side, a planner can develop the weighting system after consultation with experienced people from different spheres of administration as well as knowledgeable persons belonging to the project area. Once, the framework is designed, the arithmetical calculation is simple. A case study is presented by way of illustration in the next chapter utilising the data collected from Pursura block.

REFERENCES

1. Report of the Chief Engineers on Road Development For India (1961-81), 1958.
2. Report of the Committee on Rural Roads, 1967.
3. A.A. Walters — The Economics of Road User Charges.
4. For a full fledged description of the technique refer to The Economic Analysis of Rural Road Projects, World Bank Staff Working Paper No. 241, Annexure - 3.

6

SCREENING A NETWORK PLAN

Project Area

The project area chosen for applying the screening criterion is our old Pursurah Block in Hooghly District where the regression technique has already been experimented (Ch.-4). The existing road network was by no means adequate, considering the high density of population and relatively high output level of commercial crops. The block, as we have already seen, has an area of 100.5 Sq. Km., comprising fifty villages within it. Seven alignments of pucca road are seen on the road map supplied by Executive Engineer PW (Roads), Hooghly District. The names and road lengths are given in Table 6.1 :

Table 6.1

S. No.	*Name of the Road*	*Road Length (in Km.)*	
1.	Saidpur - Khusiganj	12.8	
2.	Pursurah - Radhanagar	8.5	
3.	Balarampur - Chatrasali	6.4	
4.	Pursurah - Arambag	5.9	
5.	Saota - Basdhuguri	6.4	(Approx.)
6.	Saidpur - Purburista	8.3	"
7.	Sahapur - Pursurah	13.0	"
	Total	61.3	"

(In the subsequent analysis, instead of names, we shall make use of serial nos. only. The roads are also numbered on the map).

The aggregate length of all the seven roads taken together is 61 Km. out of which 33.6 Km. of pucca road was complete. The main arterial, a state highway (Road No. 4 in the map and list) constructed in 1958, cuts the block just through the middle of it in east-west direction. Till early seventies, this was the only pucca road in the block, the length of the section lying within it being 5.95 Km. only. During the seventies two roads were constructed to the south of this road one of which started directly from the arterial. To the north of it, the road under construction during late seventies also started from the same arterial. With the completion of construction of this road, the total road length (pucca) would be 33.6 Km. i.e. roughly .34 per square Km. of area. A close scrutiny of the area map suggests that while a few more roads can still be constructed the layout of three roads planned for construction (one in the northern and two in the southern side of the arterial) suggests that when completed the seven roads together will form a well knit network for different villages within the block. With these roads the penetration would go up to .61 Km. per Sq.Km. of area. Road construction poses difficulty because of innumerable rivulets and nullahs abounding the area for which bridges and culverts are to be constructed. Moreover, these are almost always in spate during rainy season, rendering communication difficult.

Area of Influence of a Road Section

Whereas, the choice of alignment in respect of the arterial is to be made with reference to much wider framework than an administrative block, there should be clear cut flexible screening criterion in respect of feeder roads within a much more restricted frame of reference. An elaborate calculation of benefit cost ratios or internal rates of return with road user benefits at the base is too expensive, time consuming and at the same time often quite off the mark. However, a choice criterion is as much necessary here as in the case of arterials. Apparently the farm to market roads can easily be justified since it is a recognised fact that ease and cost of mobility have something to do with market extension and hence adds to production incentive. The

Ellet Model of Walters referred to in the previous chapter gives the idea in a nutshell. But further elaboration is needed if a comprehensive idea is to be conveyed.

What happens if we are to devise a priority list for seven road sections running through the block, as shown in the map. One of these (Road No. 4) a section of state highway may be regarded as the arterial, while others are evidently feeder roads. The first step in such an analysis is to demarcate the area of influence to each road section. The area of influence of a rural road may be defined as the area served, impacted or modified by a road in its immediate geographical environs. There are various methods of determining area of influence of a road section and accordingly the magnitude of recommended catchment area varies from case to case. In this exposition the area of influence of the arterial is taken to be extending upto two miles or a little over 3 Km. on either side of the road. From a distance beyond that limit freight traffic consisting of low value, bulky articles does not generate normally. And in our project area movement of this type of good predominates. For the three proposed roads, the area of influence is decided after taking into consideration the existing network and their usages i.e. what the villages nearer to these roads than the already existing ones, are likely to choose if they are provided with these new facilities. Villagewise data on area output, input etc. for the year 1977-78 were collected from different sources mentioned earlier. These are cumulated according to selected area of influence for each road.

Projection of Factor Values

Let us cite two examples of how this has been done. Future agricultural production and future employment in non-agriculture sector are two factors enlisted in the exposition. Value of agricultural production is estimated below.

For obtaining future projection we have made use of the regression equation relating to agriculture production developed in Chapter 4 i.e. Y = 1202 + 85.01L + 3286.879- 47r. The new roads are expected to increase penetration by 80 per cent and accordingly it is assumed that agriculture production is likely to increase by 47 x .8 = 37.6 times.

Table 6.2 : Agriculture Production in 1977-78

Road No.	*No. of villages* within area of influence*	*Per acre value of total agriculture production (Rs.)*	*Per village per acre value (Rs.)*
1	27	62994.02	2333.11
2	13	38456.27	2958.17
3	11	33118.60	3010.78
4	20	57394.74	2869.73
5	11	31028.67	2820.78
6	12	35113.46	2926.12
7	10	31241.22	3124.12

*NB : It includes villages situated both within and outside the block.

Table 6.3 : Per Acre Value of Agriculture Production is Estimated Thus

Road No.	*Projected value of agriculture production*	
	Per acre value X 37.6 (original)	*Per acre value (estimated)*
1	2333.11	87724.00
2	2958.17	111227.19
3	3010.78	113205.33
4	2869.73	107901.85
5	2820.78	106061.32
6	2926.12	110022.11
7	3124.12	117466.91

Similarly the equation for occupation structure NW = .37 - 8.12 AW - 16SC - 3.00r, gives an increase by 3 x .8 = 2.4 of non-agricultural worker consequent on 80 per cent increase in penetration.

Table 6.4 : Estimate for Non-agriculture Worker

Road No.	*Total worker in area of influence*	*p.c. of NW in 1979*	*p.c. of NW in projected case*	*Total NW*
1	14369	.22	.53	7616
2	10990	.20	.48	5275
3	10780	.24	.58	6252
4	14342	.25	.60	8605
5	4311	.21	.50	2155
6	10859	.19	.46	4995
7	10170	.23	.55	5593

Choice of Factors and Weights

The factors are selected keeping an eye to the characteristics of the region as well as to the availability of data and information. The weightage system is devised on specific consideration of the area concerned. Sometimes, one factor unit is broken into parts to accommodate varieties in the same unit. The system devised is placed in Table 6.5.

The factors can clearly be divided into two groups quantitative and qualitative, the first five items falling into the first category, while the last four into the second. In a thickly populated agricultural area, the relevance of road is mainly how it brings more people and more farms under its coverage. But other factors have to be considered also. For example, cost of providing the facility is an important factor. But since we do not have any cost estimates for the proposed roads, this important factor is left out in this analysis. On the other hand, we have taken into consideration the need for bridging as also the existence of parallel road facilities which have implications on the cost side. For treating potential perishable food product quantity of output is not available. Therefore we have accepted the main productive resource, instead of output as our selected factor. Under connectivity, we have separately treated three nodal centres, since for the area under consideration, no two of them coincide.

Table 6.5 : The Rating Scheme

S. No.	*Factors*	*Measuring Units*	*Range of Values*	*Common Rating Scale*
1	Population Served Per km. of Roads	No. of Persons per km.	0-10,000	0 - 100
2	Net Cultivated Area Served Per Km. of Road	Acres of Land Per Km. of Road	0-1,000	0 - 100
3	Furture Agriculture Production	Per Acre Value of Output to be Produced Within the Area of Influence	0 - 1,00,000	0 - 100
4	Perishable Food Production - Fish	No. of Nets and Boats	0 - 1,000	0 - 100
5	Future Employment in Non-Agriculture Sector	No. of Persons	0 - 1,000	0 - 100
6	Connectivity			
a.	Market Centre	i) Lying on the Road	Acceptance of One of these Three Alternatives	100 - 50.0
b.	Administrative	ii) Connecting the Road on Which it lies		100 - 50.0
c.	Urban Centre	No Connection		100.50.0
7	Existence of Parallel Road	At a Distance of		
		i) Above 5 km ii) Within 5 Km. iii) Within 2 km.	Acceptance of Any One of the Three Alternatives	100.50.0
8	Bridging Needed	i) None ii) One iii) More than One	Acceptance of Any One of the Three Alternatives	100.50.0
9	Existence of Other Transport Facilities	i) None ii) Waterways iii) Railways	Acceptance of Any One of the Three Alternatives	100.50.0

Once the factors are decided upon, the next step is to assign weight to each of them. This is provided in Table 6.6.

Table 6.6 : Relative Weights for Factors[1]

S. No.	*Factors*		*Factor Weights (Percentages)*
1	Population per km.		15
2	Net Cultivated Area Per Km.		10
3	Future Agriculture Production		20
4	Perishable Food Production		5
5	Future Employment in non-agriculture sector		10
6	Connectivity	a. Market Centre	5
		b. Administrative Centre	5
		c. Urban Centre	5
7	Existence of parallel road		5
8	Bridging needed		10
9	Existence of other transport facilities		10
			100

Weighted Rating

Finally, let us see what happens to the priority rating of seven roads, once we get the factor values corresponding to the area of influence of each road section and apply the factor weights for the final assessment. These factor values correspond to the area of influence of each particular road section. The reference period is 1977-78 for basic area and output figure. Next projections have been made in respect of output and employment, using the regression coefficients of yield and employment functions as has been shown earlier. The new roads will increase penetration by 80 per cent and we have assumed accordingly that the distance from pucca road will be reduced by 4/5th of the original distance. In fact, more facilities should be provided in areas where future possibilities are otherwise greater. In case of fish, we have not taken recourse to forecasting. Fish being a perishable product, people will be encouraged to catch more fish if prospect of marketability increases. Hence villages having the basic inputs nets and boats already in their possession receive greater weightage. Similarly, 1971 census figures have been accepted in the case of population on the ground that it is expected to follow the normal trend. The area being compact, movement of people between villages within it is not likely. Moreover, the density being already high compared to the district's density of rural population small improvement in roads will not encourage migration into the area. For the rest of the items we have chosen from alternative possibilities and imputed values to them since they are not ordinarily quantifiable. Table 6.7 gives details of factor values. The factor values are finally converted to common rating scale and weighted in Table 4, arrive at final priority ranking.

From Table 6.8 it appears, that highest priority is to be attached to Road No. 4 — the arterial mentioned earlier, followed by Road No. 1 and Road No. 6. Incidentally it may be pointed out that Road No. 6 is a continuation of Road No. 1 and the two together can provide a continuous north-south connection to the Block. Alongwith Road No. 4 which stretches in east-west direction, they will provide cross-wise connection to all villages. Leaving Road No. 4 aside, we find the priority ranking of rest of the roads is like this 1, 6, 7, 3, 2, 5. However, when Road Nos. 3 and 2 have already been constructed Road No. 1 is under construction and Road Nos. 6 and 7 have not been taken up at all. If there is any resource constraint then instead of taking up Road Nos. 3 and 2 at the first stage and deferring the construction of Road Nos. 5 and 7 for much later period, Road No. 1 and 6 should have been constructed first. This is an indication, that project screening is desirable at pre-execution stage.

Scope of the Method

The criterion developed so far may appear to be too simple and flexible. Reducing all the values to common rating scale, removes complexities in calculation without interfering with the effect of the factors to be distorted in the final analysis. The entire exercise can be carried on with slender data and infor-

Table 6.7 : Factor Values Accruing to Different Road Section

Road No.	Factor Values										
	1 (No.)	2 (acr)	3* (Rs.)	4 (No.)	5** (No.)	6 a	6 b	6 c	7	8	9
1.	3184	585	87724	147	7616	ii)	ii)	ii)	i)	i)	i)
2.	3189	540	111227	104	5275	ii)	ii)	ii)	ii)	ii)	ii)
3.	4060	704	113205	71	6252	iii)	iii)	iii)	iii)	i)	i)
4.	6490	1000	107901	577	8605	i)	i)	i)	i)	iii)	i)
5.	1940	478	106061	126	2156	ii)	ii)	ii)	iii)	i)	ii)
6.	3204	512	110022	85	4995	ii)	ii)	ii)	ii)	i)	i)
7.	2000	363	117466	69	5593	ii)	ii)	ii)	ii)	i)	i)

* The increase in the value of future output is estimated to be 37.6.

** The increase in future proportion of non agriculture labour is estimated separately for each Road Section.

Note : For qualitative factors 6, 7, 8, 9 refer to Table-1, Col. 3.

Table 6.8 : Rating of Roads Within the Project Area

Sl. No.	*Factor Weight*	*Ratings*							*Weighted Ratings*						
		Road No.							*Road No.*						
		1	2	3	4	5	6	7	1	2	3	4	5	6	7
1	.15	32	32	40	65	19	32	20	4.80	4.80	6.00	9.75	2.85	4.80	3.00
2	.10	58	54	70	100	48	51	36	5.80	5.40	7.00	10.00	4.80	5.10	3.60
3	.20	87	111	113	108	106	110	117	17.40	22.20	22.60	21.60	21.20	22.00	23.40
4	.05	15	10	7	58	13	8	7	.75	.50	.35	2.90	.65	.40	.35
5	.10	76	53	62	86	21	50	56	7.60	5.30	6.20	8.60	2.10	5.00	5.60
6a	.05	50	50	0	100	50	50	50	2.50	2.50	0.00	5.00	2.50	2.50	2.50
b	.05	50	50	0	100	50	50	50	2.50	2.50	0.00	5.00	2.50	2.50	2.50
c	.05	50	50	0	100	50	50	50	2.50	2.50	0.00	5.00	2.50	2.50	2.50
7	.05	100	50	0	100	0	50	50	5.00	2.50	0.00	5.00	0.00	2.50	2.50
8	.10	100	50	100	0	100	100	100	10.00	5.00	10.00	0.00	10.00	10.00	10.00
9	.10	100	50	100	100	50	100	100	10.00	5.00	10.00	10.00	5.00	10.00	10.00
	100								68.85	58.20	62.15	82.85	54.10	67.30	65.95

mation. In fact, some sort of rational judgement can be formulated with whatever factual basis one can lay hands upon. It does not require the expertise and elaborate data base of social cost benefit analysis. But essentially it takes into consideration both cost and benefit for project selection. Specially, in the benefit side its coverage is quite significant in so far as it treats tangible and non-tangible benefits on the same footing.

But the limitation of the technique lies in its flexibility. For evaluation purposes it is always desirable to deduce a uniform criterion. Since one can have enough independence in choosing factors and weights the variability itself may lead to inconsistent formulation of the criterion. Moreover, the weighting system is purely psychological and is therefore exposed to the risk of inviting personal bias. The choice of area of influence offers another hurdle. Naturally, the areas are quite often overlapping and one cannot be sure about the share of influence of one or other of the road on a particular area.

In conclusion, it may be suggested that even though we may try our best, we are not in a position to arrive at a model of universal application for selecting road projects. For example, this particular model is not to be recommended for evaluating high way projects where traffic is heavy, diversified and transport engineers and economists have arrived at a fairly satisfactory level of expertise for quantifying road user benefit. This method, however, can easily be tried for determining construction priorities of rural roads whose socio-economic importance is great for the area while their potentiality for generating fast moving traffic is limited.

REFERENCES

1. The weighting system follows the pattern provided in Stanley's article with adjustments suited to our project area :- W.R. Stanley—Evaluating Construction Priorities of Farm to Market Roads in Developing Countries -*The Journal of Developing Areas*, April 1971, Vol. 5, No. 3.

PART IV

SOME STRAY THOUGHTS ON RURAL TRANSPORT

7

WATER TRANSPORT IN RURAL ECONOMY

Feasibility of Water Transport

We have so far concentrated on road as a means of communication in rural areas and studied road projects from different standpoint. At the same time we admit that water transport also plays a significant role when the natural advantages are in existence. From a definitional point of view inland waterways comprise within it rivers, canals, backwaters, lakes and creeks. But in order that the waterways may be usable throughout the year they must have a specific depth and continuous flow.

Now people normally have a preference for road transport because of speed and relatively easy accessibility. Once a land route is developed it generates new traffic, but this is not always true in case of water transport. In order that water transport may become viable three conditions should always be fulfilled. First, there is to be an assured navigable channel round the year with minimum required draft. Secondly, there should be adequate infrastructural facilities at terminal points for loading/unloading of cargoes and embarking/disembarking of passengers. Finally, an all time service capable of being competitive with or complementary to land transport should also be developed.

The traffic needs of a rural area is never exceptionally large. The main need is to export the surplus generated within the economy and to import inputs for raising productivity level. A low activity level obviously does not generate heavy demand for input. Water transport is best suited to carry low value high volume bulk cargoes. In rural areas of our country, this type of commodity traffic is quite common. But difficulties are there. Since the movement is rather slow, perishable commodities cannot be gainfully transported. People also do not like to make a long journey along waterways since it is time consuming and uncomfortable. For passenger traffic shoft distance ferry crossing interconnecting land routes are more popular rather than long journey along a particular route. Therefore a cautious approach is needed in this sphere, because transport services cannot be fruitfully developed unless there is enough public demand.

In the face of global difficulties concerning oil supply, water transport is often supported for being cost efficient i.e. in terms of fuel consumption. The cost of manufacturing and maintaining mechanised boats are not negligible. We do have country boats which may be compared to animal driven vehicles along land routes. Traditionally, villagers in India depend on country boats and bullock carts for moving about from place to place. Naturally, the sphere of movement is not large and frequency of movement is also quite low. Relatively rich people have their own vehicles. For example, bullock carts are used by their owners both for carrying commodity to market centre as also for making trips to nearby urban centre. Similarly a village merchant in a riverine area keeps boat for transporting his merchandise. Apart from ownership vehicles, the same types of vehicles are also available on hire. In case of ferry services though it is privately managed and operated the local government also comes into the picture.

Modes of Water Transport

Now, roads, specially pucca roads carry a relatively large variety of vehicles in rural areas. Water transport also admits of certain varieties. The traditional variety is of course the country boat made of wood. These boats will cotinue to be plied for small scale traffic and these are the only mode in shailow-water. But these have certain inherent defects and hence are not suited for large scale mechanised inland navigation, which is the need of the hour. Generally, they are built of unseasoned local wood and start leaking after little use. As a consequence, operation of bailing out water have to be carried out frequently for recaulking. Moreover, they cannot afford adequate protection to cargo against weather and pilferage. It is also slow moving. Speed is becoming a major criterion for chosing a mode of transport. Now a days in rural areas of West Bengal particularly in Sunderban area where people have to depend to a large extent on water transport, country boats are fitted with in board diesel motors. These are popularly called 'bhat bhati', because of the noise that they generate. But this is a risky device and is accident prone in turbulent rivers. Modern steel or light alloy barges are welcome in these areas, with adequate safe guards against accident.

Now vessels of different models ensuring both speed and safety are not scarce in modern society. In developed economies, people are making use of water transport in selected cases. In USA water transport is being recognised as the cheapest mode encouraging industrialisation. It has an additional advantage since the industrialists can own their own fleet at a relatively low cost and run them to suit their own convenience and requirements. This is evidently not possible in case of airways and railways. Even if a fleet of trucks may be owned, this will prove expensive in terms of both capital and running cost.

England and France make wide use of canals. In France, Seine, Meselle and some other rivers have been made navigable through construction of weirs and locks. In Germany, canals have been constructed to circumvent steep and rocky reaches of the Rhine and the Rhone to provide a better route for navigation. The canals of Amsterdam play an effective role in the city transport system. Venice is celebrated for its water transport. But all these countries make use of high standard mechanised boats. They ensure speed, safety and comfort. Therefore they can effectively supplement land routes.

If we are to develop water transport in our country new models have to be adopted. We have to switch over to mechanised transport. The capacity of the vessel will have to be determined by the traffic that it expects to bear and the navigability of the waterways. Steps should also be taken to enhance navigability by restoring different methods adopted in developed countries. An effective utilisation of waterways also requires large scale hydrographic surveys. But natural advantage for using mechanised vessels is limited in this country.

Importance of Waterways in India

The inland water transport system played an important role in the early history of India. Long before the introduction of the railways, inland water transport was the life line of the country. The Ganges and Yamuna in the north and the Godavari, the Normoda and the Tapti in the south were widely used for commercial navigation. Towards the end of 19th Century, we find evidences of heavy traffic along river Hooghly. However, with the growth of railways its importance declined and many routes went out of use.

In the present era, the importance of waterways is again recognised and the need for developing the system is being emphasised, particularly from the sixth plan period. Ten major rivers and canals have been declared national waterways. An agency, the Inland Waterways Authority of India was created in 1985 to look after national waterways. The IWAI is to develop, maintain and also administer the national waterways mainly from the point of view of shipping and navigation. Other uses like supply of drinking water, irrigation, power generation do not come under its purview. The IWAI in its turn appointed a Committee which is to prepare a master plan for IWT till 2000 A.D. A high level committee has also been constituted to formulate the basic policy of developing and maintaining the waterways in the country.

According to the National Transport Policy Committee Report, the navigable length of inland waterways in India is 14544 kms. out of which 4303 kms. run along canals and 10241 kms. run along rivers. The density of navigable waterways per 100 sq.km. of area is .44 km. only. Now of these total length of waterways, 5,200 kms. of major rivers and 485 kms. of canals are suitable for mechanised crafts. But only a stretch of 1799 kms. along rivers and another strech of 231 kms. along canals are actually utilised by mechanised vessels. The IWAI is naturally interested in major routes. Mainly cargo movements take place along long routes covering more than one State. For example Allahabad (UP) - Haldia (West Bengal) strech of Ganga-Bhagirathi-Hooghly river has been declared a national waterway and the Central Govt. is made responsible for utilising the waterway. A regular cargo movement by IWT between Haldia and Patna has started since 1987. The Central Inland Water Corporation, a Govt. of India undertaking was set up at Calcutta in 1967. It operates river services carrying goods between Calcutta and Assam via Bangladesh. It is also operating river services between Calcutta and Farakka as also Calcutta and Cachar (Assam).

Now, these major routes run through both urban and rural areas. But we are interested in short haulage of both goods and passengers in rural areas where navigable waterways exist. West Bengal has a good length of waterways, 2337 kms. In terms of total length it comes only next to U.P. But more important is the density per 100 sq. kms. of area. In this respect also West Bengal with a density of 2.66 km. comes third, first and second positions being occupied by Goa, Daman and Diu (9.00 km.) and Kerala (3.98 km.) respectively.

Short distance ferry services carrying both commodities passengers are in existence in West Bengal for a pretty long time. The ferries in rural areas are regulated by Bengal Ferries Act, 1885. The regulation, control and superintendence of public ferries vest with district administration and Land and Land Revenue Department used to get a lumpsum money from the operator of the service who would take the route on lease for a certain period of time. The same act provides that the public ferry may be managed by a local authority having jurisdiction over the area in which such ferry is situated. On the strength of the provision, now the Zila Parishad has come into the picture and replaced the L & L R Deptt. The ferry service is sometimes operated by the local Panchayet Samiti also. The striking feature of such ferry services is the unbelievably low fare rate. There are ferry services which charge only 5 paise per trip in a country boat. At the time of heavy excalation of transport cost, one cannot afford to dispense with such a cheap mode of transport. For example, from a particular spot of Hooghly Dt. one can cross over to another spot in North 24 Parganas by paying only 5 paise or 10 paise. The same route when covered by bus or train will cost a passenger Rs. 5 to 6. We have no exhaustive statistics of ferry services operating within the state. There must have been scope for improving the services and the appraisal techniques developed in the context of rural road may be applied in these cases as well.

A Study of Sunderbans — the Deltaic Region

A typical case for developing water transport exists in the deltaic region of Sunderbans in the south of West Bengal. Innumerable rivers, canals, creeks criss cross the region. In many areas, boats are the only means of transport. The Sunderbans has an area of 9630 sq. km. of which human habitation is found in 5367 sq. km. of area. The rest of the area is covered by thick bushes and are not fit for human settlement. In all there are fifty four islands which have been organised into fifteen administrative blocks. The area map shows the divisions. The islands are protected from innundation by a 450 km. long embankment maintained by Irrigation & Waterways Deptt. The different habitation spots are not far off from Calcutta. For example, one boundary point by sea side, -- Bakkhali - which is being developed as a tourist spot is only 123 km. from Calcutta including a short ferry crossing.

On the whole the communication system is very poor in Sunderbans. Now, water transport is convenient for moving from one island to another and road system can be improved within the island. Bus services are operating connecting the boundary points in different directions with Calcutta. Thus there are bus routes like Calcutta - Narayanpur; Calcutta - Hasanabad, Calcutta - Sonakhali. Narayanpur appears to be an important waterways junction. One can cross over to Namkhana in a country boat and then again take a journey by bus, the terminal point being Bakkhali - 18 kms. from Namkhana. Again from Narayanpur, one can make boat journeys along the river to other island points like Rakhaskhali, Buroaburi Tat, Sumati Nagar, Bakdanga. Within these islands road transports are available depending on growth of habitation and economic activities. A few medium vehicles like vans ply on some areas. But the widely used mode of transport is manually operated 3-wheeled cycle rickshaws. They carry both commodities and passengers.

From different points on Calcutta-Narayanpur Road there are several link roads leading to ferry crossing points like Harwood

Point, Raidighi etc. Ferry crossing or water routes from these spots again lead to some other human settlements in some other island. Similarly Calcutta–Sonakhali route after ferry crossing brings one to Basanti–Gosaba block areas. Within these blocks there are short water routes and land routes. The journey from Calcutta to Hemnagar in the present system involves coming to Hasanabad by bus, crossing over to the other side, then again a journey by say rickshaw upto Barunhat, a crossing, a land journey, another crossing at Hingalganja, again a land route, next a crossing from Nebukhali to Dulduli and then a journey on road up to Hemnagar. This is how one is to move within Sundarban area. I am refering only to cases where some form of communication has developed.

Naturally there is scope for making further improvement which will also have favourable impact on the economy of the area. One obvious way is to take recourse to construction of bridges on rivers and canals which will build a continuous land route. Apart from cost involved, such step may lead to ecological disturbances. Another way is to construct RCC Jetties on both sides of river/canal crossing so that people are less inconvenienced while embarking on or disembarking from vessels, retaining the water routes. If and when, natural advantages permit, barges may be made use of for carrying buses and lorries for which a more stable and expensive jetty may be needed. For example, along Hasanabad-Hemnagar route there are proposals for constructing special jetties at a cost of a little below Rs. 1 crore or Rs. 1.25 crores at crossing points on both sides. The vessels for carrying buses and trucks cost Rs. 60 lakhs at present. But though expensive this will ensure continuous journey by a single vehicle.

Thus here is a case of choice whether to build RCC jetties and make use of launch and boat services or to build special types of jetties and prepare a situation of semi land route? The cost benefit criterion can be suitably made use of to guide the choice. Along with the advantages to be derived by passengers in the form of saving in time, the reorganisation benefit expected out of ease of mobility is to be studied more deeply. It is argued that cash crop like cotton, oilseed will be grown in the area if transportation is easier. The information gap will be removed and supply of input and marketability of product will be facilitated. But a patient probing is needed to assess the possibility.

A second issue involves the choice of vessel type. Country boats are better to be replaced in near future. The most popular form 'bhootbhuti' ensures speed and hence very much liked by people in the area where travel time is a crucial factor. But the type is accident prone. There is every justification of introducing mechanised vessels and suitable types are to be devised for the purpose. Of course, cost will be higher and fares will rise. A cost effective design taking into account capacity, speed and safety consideration should have to be introduced. Technical studies have to be undertaken for the purpose.

The most logical approach is to prepare a priority list of improvement in transportation taking into account the size of investible fund in the particular sector within a given period. For example, construction of RCC jetties at ferry crossing points is an important project. The number of ferry crossing points have to be ascertained. The importance of RCC jetties will have to be examined by taking into account frequency of trips, number of average daily passenger, volume of goods movement, prospect of producing agriculture surplus in the hinterland (say, vegetables, cash crops etc.), prospect of pisciculture so forth and so on. The weighted rating method may be applied for prioritisation of schemes of jetty improvement. Thus while the role of water transport in Sunderban areas should always be recognised, sound judgement is needed for recommending specific steps in selected areas. Techno economic analysis should guide these decisions.

8

A BALANCED APPROACH TO RURAL TRANSPORT

Mobility Within Human Settlement

The analytical framework of the study hinges on the issue of choice of road project in rural area. The basic framework can be extended to water transport as well with suitable choice of indicators of benefit. Now what is to be the infrastructure in a rural area? We have to look back and study the issue with a historical perspective. While applying theoretical model to practical situation I have not changed the time sequence, since present time is not an important factor in such analysis.

The growth of human habitation depends on productive opportunity of a particular area and the spread of contact with areas offering better opportunity. Historically, settlements grew in areas with fertile land where cultivation was possible and therefore supply of basic food was asssured. The draft animals were utilised both for ploughing the fields as also for carrying men and goods to neighbouring area. In the absence of animal power, the fields used to be within reasonably convenient walking distance of owner cultivators or tenants. The tillers of the soil, the landless labourers used to throng near cultivable area in search of work opportunity. Villages thus came into existence and a class of artisans gradually made their appearance to supply other needs of the village society. The artisans were normally allotted a share of land where produce would contribute towards their maintenance. So the rural economy was land based and used to lead an isolated existence. This is the picture of old countries like India, China. The status was not much different in countries like USA, Australia where settlements grew mainly through migration. In fact fertility of land and accessibility are the two criteria for growth of settlements. The early history of growth of habitation in coastal areas testify to the fact that with the introduction of shipping as a mode of transport, people used to make oversea trips and settle by the sea side in a new country.

Now leaving aside growth of settlements we now take up the issue of movement within the settlement. As population grows, settlements are multiplied. Initially, a country nurtures small settlements i..e. villages. As villages increase in numbers their proximity to one another become a reflexion of means of transport. Thus under walk to work culture, distance between two contiguous villages will be of the orders of two to three kms. When animal driven vehicles are developed a distance of six/seven kilometres can be negotiated easily. With the advent of motor vehicles, the countries become smaller i.e. movement from place to place cease to be much of a constraints.

Now, introduction of motor vehicle is not an isolated affair. Along with it technological innovations occured in other productive sectors as well. Industrialisation, mechanisation of agriculture and such other developments changed the face of the world. The present economy is characterised by fast movement, diversified consumer budget, mechanised system of production so forth and so on.

A broad classification of rural and urban areas however persists all over the world, signifying a lower and less diversified activity level for rural areas. Hence, the need for mobility is also lower, compared to urban areas.

The Indian Scenario

Some facts about transportation in India with special reference to rural areas may be discussed at this stage since whatever analytical framework we may prepare, should be suitable for application to the Indian context. The British people laid down a fairly wide network of railway system in India. The route kilometerage under railways increased by 15.6 per cent in between 1950-51 and 1987-88. It came to 61,976 kms. on March 1988 of which 8,157 km have been electrified. Goods traffic has a major share contributing 74 per cent of total traffic earnings to railway coffer. In recent years there is a major shift of passenger traffic in favour of roads. The share of passenger traffic in total land routes went up from 26 per cent in 1950-51 to 78 per cent in 1987-88. While railways cater to long distance traffic, highways play a competitive or complementary role and organise point to point services.

India has built up on extensive road network since independence. The system has been organised to act as a feeder to railway terminals, ports and harbours. In rural areas roads are sometimes the only means of transport. The road length increased by 343 p.c. from 1950-51 to 1984-85, the total length being 1,772,000 kms. in 1984-85. It includes all administrative categories of roads like national highways, state highways, district roads, project roads etc. 47 p.c. of the total road length is surfaced. The following table gives an idea of penetration of road network in rural areas.

Accessibility of Villages with Roads, March End 1985

Population Category	*Total No. of Villages*	*No. of villages connected as on March end 1985*	*Col. (2) as a % of Col. (3)*
1,500 & above	69,408	48,921	70.5
1,000 - 1,500	56,609	28,967	51.2
less than 1,000	4,66,075	1,24,611	26.7
Total	5,92,092	2,02,499	34.2

Thus, the state is giving effect to its objective enumerated in 5th and 6th five year plans.

The importance of inland waterways is negligible in quantitative terms. It constitutes just one per cent of the entire transport system of the country. The total navigable inland waterways come to nearly 14,544 kms. Out of this length only 5,200 kms. of major rivers and 485 kms. of canals are suitable for operation of mechanised crafts as has been already pointed out. The importance of waterways comes not from stretch of the area that it serves but from the significant part that it can play in selected areas, one of them the Sunderbans' has already provided a good example.[1]

The Government has from time to time appointed expert committees to formulate an overall transport policy or to review problems of particular section. For example an one man Rural Road Development Committee was appointed in 1968 which submitted its report, giving its views on formation of a road network at the district level. Various studies suggesting suitable road network plan for rural areas were developed during the seventies.

A National Transport Policy Committee submitted its report in 1980 projecting the future development in transportation network. According to this report, the passenger rail traffic is expected to double and freight traffic, more than double in between 1977-78 and 2000 A.D. According to the same report, mechanised road transport would increase from 77 billion ton km. and 250 billion passengers kms. to 1,982 billion ton kms. and 800 billion passenger kms. respectively during the same period. These projections were based on mathematical models of past economic trends and transport demand relationship. Five years later, the Planning Commission set up another Steering Committee for Transport Planning to evolve a perspective plan for transport sector. Thus there is no dirth of studies in the sphere.

A Co-ordinated Approach at the Micro Level

While such studies may be helpful for overall policy formulation, more specific approach is needed in case of area development plan. Rural transport is to be viewed as providing a basic infrastructure in a particular area. Now as has been already pointed out the transport network in rural area provides inter connection between growth centres and human settlements. The growth centres may be of different order. Normally the link with a growth centre is vital for the village economy.

Railways running through the length and breadth of the country do pass through rural areas. But the layout is such as to connect important towns lying at a sufficiently long distance from one another. On the way the railways also touch rural or semi urban points. But they are fed by local services which are not frequent. Say one or two locomotives touch the point throughout the day. Even then people have to move in ward from railheads. There in road transport comes to the picture. In fact road network can penetrate remote areas and can carry different types of vehicles, which is a distinct advantage for rural areas. Water transport also plays a significant role in selected areas. Thus while planning a transport network for rural areas, the three routes are to be made use of simultaneously depending on natural advantage, cost consideration and demand for a particular transport service.

The task before a planner is to maximise an objective function under certain constraints. While trying to maximise the objective function, the planner has to come down to the micro level for the gap between planning and performance sometimes becomes too large at the project level. Though planning is a more or less centralised process, decentralisation is called for to ensure efficiency. A plan is a balanced conglomeration of projects. The success of the plan will depend on proper choice of projects and each one of the projects should contribute to the ultimate objective of the plan. Thus if the objective of a transport planner in rural area is to maximise the degree of penetration with a given level of investment he should try to increase connectivity i.e. provide connections to as many habitation points as possible. If the objective is to harness a scarce resource lying in an obscure area then the link of this point with important growth centres will have to be improved.

The advantage at the project level lies in the fact that objective function can be interpreted in a more concrete form, choice variables are not so numerous. Hence a planner is in a better position at the micro level to control the choice variables and maximise the objective function.

The micro level planning in transport sector starts within a compact area — say a block which is the lowest administrative unit in our country. The natural condition and existing facilities are studied first. Normally, the block headquarter is selected to be a place where some infrastructural facilities are already there. The connection between the headquarter and villages within the block is to be strengthened first. The block headquarter is often situated on a railhead or by the side of an arterial or on a important ferry crossing where water routes are quite important. So when villages are connected with block headquarters they have access to an important nodal point. But this is not the only objective. Villages lying further off from the headquarter may be nearer to the headquarters of adjacent block or a market centre. Interconnections may be developed that way also.

The choice of alignments, the mode of transport, the frequency of service all these are crucial variables. The analytical techniques developed and illustrated in this work may be applied to arrive at a balanced transport network in a compact rural area. The choice may take different angles choice of alignment within a particular sector say road, choice between two different routes — say between roadway and railway, or between roadway and waterway, choice of a particular vehicle type along a route so forth and so on. The crucial point is always identification and quantification of benefit to be derived from a particular project. They can be pinpointed through regression analysis establishing relationship between an independent and a set of explanatory variables. When a high level of sophistication cannot be reached at least some items may be identified which are likely to be affected by improvement in transport and the logic of transport planning in rural area may be developed along that line.

REFERENCES

1. N.B. : The figures quoted in the Section are taken from Basic Statistics Relating to the Indian Economy, Vol. I, All India, August 1989, CMIE, Bombay.

APPENDICES

Appendix I
(Chapter 2)

Table 1 : Benefit Estimates Per Mile of M.K.M.M. Road Sum Total of Discounted Value of Benefit for Different Time Periods.

$B_t (1 + i)^{-t}$, *Where* t = n+3

	Case I			*Case II*		
e/i	8	10	12	8	10	12
			Single Income Estimate			
1	538721.76	434802.07	355767.80	611760.21	491589.54	400587.34
1.5	540470.99	436031.99	356790.52	613518.84	493002.71	401738.91
1.7	541211.49	436649.42	357279.36	614359.41	493678.17	402289.33
			n = 20			
1	670796.40	513641.95	403466.31	743634.86	570429.43	448285.86
1.5	672724.74	515118.51	404626.16	745772.58	572069.23	449574.54
1.7	673646.43	515824.27	405180.53	746794.36	572853.02	450190.50
			n = 30			
1	752887.49	554491.88	424105.71	802510.65	599769.51	463130.75
1.5	755051.81	556085.88	425324.88	804817.62	601493.66	464462.11
1.7	756086.30	556847.77	425907.62	805920.29	602317.77	465098.46
			n =40			
			Differential Income Estimate			
1	691006.04	557503.66	456165.84	784399.58	630316.62	513633.50
1.5	692555.36	558753.66	457188.62	786158.31	631729.88	514785.14
1.7	693295.86	559351.09	457677.46	786998.89	632405.34	515335.56
			n = 20			
1	860095.84	658592.24	517324.93	953489.38	731405.20	574792.59
1.5	862024.29	660068.89	518484.84	955627.23	733045.11	576081.35
1.7	862945.99	660774.65	519039.21	956649.01	733823.90	576697.31
			n = 30			
1	965353.11	710970.06	543788.77	1028980.00	769025.08	593826.72
1.5	967517.57	712564.16	545008.02	1031287.10	770749.34	595158.16
1.7	968552.06	713326.05	545590.76	1032389.80	771573.45	595794.52
			n = 40			

Table 2 : Investment Cost Per Mile of M.K.M.M. Road at Different Rates of Interest and Different Values of Exchange Rate

$$\sum_{t=1}^{q} K_t (1+i)^{-t} \quad \textit{Where } q = 3$$

e/i	*8*	*10*	*12*
(1)	(2)	(3)	(4)
1.00	74613.41	72241.30	69995.92
1.50	77055.32	74605.56	72286.69
1.70	78032.07	75551.27	73203.00

Table 3 : Maintenance Costs Per Mile of M.K.M.M. Road at Different Rates of Interest, at Different Time Interval.

$$O\,\Sigma(1+i)^{-t} \quad t = n + 3$$

t/i	*8*	*10*	*12*
(1)	(2)	(3)	(4)
20	37510.07	30781.05	25586.15
30	43010.02	34083.16	27590.02
40	45557.54	35356.25	28236.01

Appendix II
(Chapter 4) (31st.)
Micro Level Data For Regression Analysis

S. No.	Name of the Village	Population 1971	Total Workers	Persons engaged in agriculture	Gross area under Cultivation (acres)	Gross area under Irrigation (acres)	Area (acres) under Agril. Potato	Jute	Puddy	output Qtl. Potato	Jute	Prices per Qtl. (Rs.) Potato	Jute	Distance of village from nearest pucca road (km)	Total value of Agriculture Output. (Rs.)
1	2	3	4	5	6	7	8	9	10	11	12	13	14	15	16
1.	Sahapur	1,499	232	214	680	355	180	70	300	14400	420	30	150	12.44	2034600
2.	Bhangamore	1,808	400	246	760	415	220	70	340	17600	560	30	150	11.83	2480280
3.	Krishnabullavpur	1,215	392	326	700	370	190	70	310	12350	560	32	160	10.24	1990030
4.	Soaluk	4,526	1158	882	2580	1475	820	210	1160	59040	1470	32	160	9.60	7995756
5.	Baikunthapur	5,074	1573	968	1980	1145	620	170	890	44640	1360	33	165	8.80	6370320
6.	Kolepu	2,221	536	452	875	530	250	70	370	15000	560	28	150	8.00	2460900

(Contd.)

1	2	3	4	5	6	7	8	9	10	11	12	13	14	15	16
7.	Dulalbah	698	174	94	278	125	50	40	120	3600	240	28	150	7.68	658160
8.	Ranabagpur	1,176	337	258	470	195	120	50	210	9600	400	30	150	7.20	1477660
9.	Krishnabati	1,059	233	191	161	75	30	30	70	3150	240	30	155	6.40	510770
10.	Baitha	997	262	230	490	250	130	50	220	9100	300	32	155	5.92	1367840
11.	Kulpatpur	2,341	728	623	750	405	220	70	340	17600	560	32	160	5.92	2532320
12.	Dihipatpur	1,902	881	703	710	375	200	70	320	16000	.420	33	160	5.60	2211400
13.	Deulpara	1,278	607	490	470	245	120	50	210	9600	300	33	173	6.40	1410300
14.	Alati	1,759	821	647	470	235	120	50	210	8640	350	35	173	3.80	1395138
15.	Rasulpur	1,859	864	679	710	385	200	70	320	14400	560	35	173	3.20	2198140
16.	Paschimpara	3,112	1847	1494	670	355	180	70	300	12960	560	40	180	.20	2030560
17.	Harimakhali	1,397	389	352	510	275	140	50	230	11200	300	35	165	4.48	1642470
18.	Rasik Chalk	218	128	87	268	115	50	40	120	4000	280	37	175	.80	780920

19.	Takipur	1,091	509	412	268	115	50	40	120	4000	240	38	175	1.20	689720
20.	Nimalangi	2,552	1189	954	750	405	220	70	340	17600	490	40	180	.20	2393086
21.	Jangalpara	5,672	2500	2045	2015	985	620	170	900	55800	1020	40	180	.50	7291350
22.	Pursura	3,985	1900	1440	1040	570	300	100	470	24000	600	40	180	.40	3252340
23.	Harihar	1,497	435	348	470	245	120	50	210	8400	300	40	180	.20	1251020
24.	Srirampur	4,493	1179	948	1410	790	420	140	640	31920	840	40	180	.10	4149480
25.	Rautara	2,298	546	437	750	415	220	70	340	15400	630	40	180	.80	2133880
26.	Saidpur	2,922	1109	887	470	245	120	50	210	9600	250	40	180	.20	1318676
27.	Marinan	1,936	502	322	670	355	180	70	300	14400	420	40	180	.80	1986980
28.	Saota	1,388	368	256	1120	620	330	100	410	23100	700	39	180	1.20	3228520
29.	Kadipur	235	128	96	170	90	40	20	80	2720	140	39	180	1.92	539400
30.	Bheuta	935	207	150	370	200	1000	40	170	6500	240	28	160	3.68	983410

(Contd.)

1	2	3	4	5	6	7	8	9	10	11	12	13	14	15	16
31.	Bhungera	4,002	476	379	348	185	90	40	160	6120	260	32	165	2.88	919740
32.	Samaspur	471	120	114	465	245	120	50	210	8160	300	32	165	2.72	1227430
33.	Hati	2,292	728	633	695	370	190	70	310	13300	420	36	170	1.92	1919740
34.	Parul	791	392	315	283	140	60	40	130	4320	280	40	173	.80	540430
35.	Balarampur	1,556	430	396	503	275	140	50	230	10080	350	40	180	.20	1453030
36.	Sundarus	1,385	632	505	363	200	100	40	170	8500	200	38	173	.20	1133850
37.	Hetamchak	959	438	349	280	140	60	40	130	4800	200	37	165	7.00	732850
38.	Akrifatepur	2735	1157	939	1120	610	340	100	510	23800	600	35	165	8	3415760
39.	Chillidanga	4317	1898	1508	779	530	230	70	350	25700	490	40	180	8	3251420
40.	Harma	996	458	360	322	170	80	40	150	6400	320	40	180	11	927530

41.	Benegachi	801	377	282	322	170	80	40	150	6000	320	32	160	11	917920
42.	Gasar	801	369	269	302	155	70	40	140	4900	320	32	160	9	816720
43.	Gobindapur	1,202	534	429	958	530	230	100	440	1960	800	40	180	11	2889530
44.	Baradiguri	2,249	978	770	900	485	250	100	410	21250	900	38	178	13	2797660
45.	Gholadiguri	3,037	1408	1124	1270	710	380	120	580	30400	600	40	180	14	3889960
46.	Neota	1,183	552	449	482	256	120	60	220	9600	300	38	178	10	1337110
47.	Syampur	3,671	1682	336	1665	930	500	170	760	40000	650	30	165	12	4919620
48.	Parbhuristha	1,033	472	388	342	175	80	50	160	6800	250	28	160	8	323520
49.	Kotalpara	1,509	583	469	537	280	140	60	240	11200	240	28	160	11	1482590
50.	Parshaympur	1,664	779	626	492	260	130	50	220	11050	250	30	165	9	1452810

N.B. : The Yield and Area Figures are for 1977-78. Others data refer to March or June 1979.

INDEX